Published by: Kansas City Star Books
1729 Grand Blvd.
Kansas City, Missouri, USA 64108

First edition, first printing
ISBN: 9781935362364

Library of Congress Control Number:
2009924512

Printed in the United States of America by Walsworth Publishing Co., Marceline, Missouri

To order copies, call toll-free 866-834-7467.

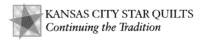

KANSAS CITY STAR QUILTS
Continuing the Tradition

The Quilter's Home Page

www.PickleDish.com
www.PickleDishStore.com

My Stars III

Patterns from The Kansas City Star • Volume III

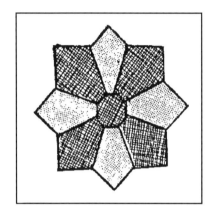

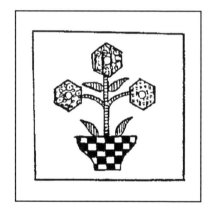

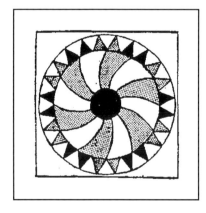

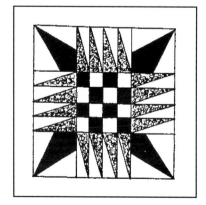

Here we are again with our third installment of the *My Stars: Patterns from The Kansas City Star* series. This volume includes a variety of patterns, from the simple – such as Thrifty and Roman Stripe – to the more difficult – such as Wagon Wheels and Heart's Desire. The patterns originally hailed from readers of the historical Kansas City Star newspaper, from Hugo, Colo., to Hunter, Ark. All 25 patterns are inspiring in their uniqueness and place in history.

Also included are photographs of quilts from people just like you – our readers and quilt enthusiasts. Once again, we have a beautiful selection of quilts from the past, as well as updated versions. These quilt photos match the patterns in the book, so you'll get to see ways in which actual quilts are made up using the patterns.

The Kansas City Star began printing traditional quilt patterns in 1928. The patterns were a weekly feature in The Star or its sister publications, The Weekly Star and The Star Farmer, from 1928 until the mid-1930s, then less regularly until 1961. By the time the last one ran, more than 1,000 had been published in the papers, which circulated in seven Midwestern states as well as North Carolina, Kentucky and Texas.

In the fall of 1999, The Star reprinted a few dozen of the patterns as a book to test the continued popularity of the patterns. The 5,000-book printing sold out in less than two weeks. Thus, Kansas City Star Quilts was born.

The Kansas City Star patterns continue to pop up in books, but Star Quilts has never put together a complete volume of all of the blocks. So in August 2007, it launched a program called My Star Collection. Each week, a redraft of an old pattern that was published in the newspaper is offered to My Star Collection subscribers. This program will continue until all 1,000+ patterns are redrafted.

This book is comprised of 25 of the patterns that were offered to My Star Collection subscribers. Each pattern includes fabric requirements, templates and assembly instructions, as well as the original caption that was printed in the newspaper.

So whether you plan to stitch these famous old blocks or are a collector, sit back and enjoy the heritage of quilting. And clear a spot on your shelf, because eventually Kansas City Star Quilts will chronicle them all. This is still just the beginning.

Diane McLendon
Editor

* * *

Kansas City Star Quilts would like to thank the hard-working team that has made My Star Collection and the *My Stars* series possible: Edie McGinnis, Jenifer Dick, Kim Walsh, Doug Weaver, Aaron Leimkuehler, Jo Ann Groves, Christina DeArmond and of course, our subscribers and quilt friends who have graciously provided their quilts to be included in this book.

* * *

My Star Collection is a weekly subscription service where subscribers download a pdf pattern – from The Kansas City Star's historical 1928 to 1961 collection – each week. The subscription is for a year of patterns – 52 in all. For more information or to sign up, visit subscriptions.pickledish.com.

TABLE OF CONTENTS

8-Point Snowflake

Block Size: 12" finished

Fabric needed

Light blue

Medium blue

Dark blue

We'll use templates because of the oddly shaped pieces.

Cutting directions

From light blue, cut

8 pieces using template A

From the medium blue, cut

4 pieces using template B

From the dark blue, cut

4 pieces using template C

1 circle using template D

8-Point Snowflake

To Make the Block

1 Sew the B and C pieces into two sets of four as shown. Don't sew all the way to the end of the seams as they will be inset later.

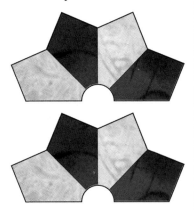

2 Join the two sets.

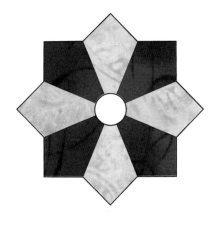

3 Add the A pieces. Sew in the directions of the arrows then miter the seam where the two A pieces meet.

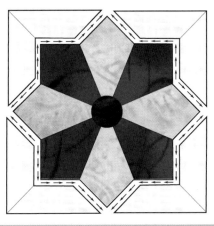

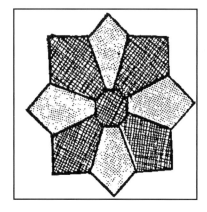

Appliqué the D circle in place to complete the block.

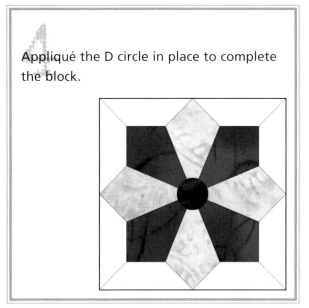

From The Kansas City Star, April 8, 1953:

No. 921

Alternate print and 1-tone blocks, or an alternating arrangement of very small prints with checks or plaids is pleasing for the 8-Point Snowflake. The pattern is a contribution of Mrs. Bob Mullinax, route 1, Farmington, Mo.

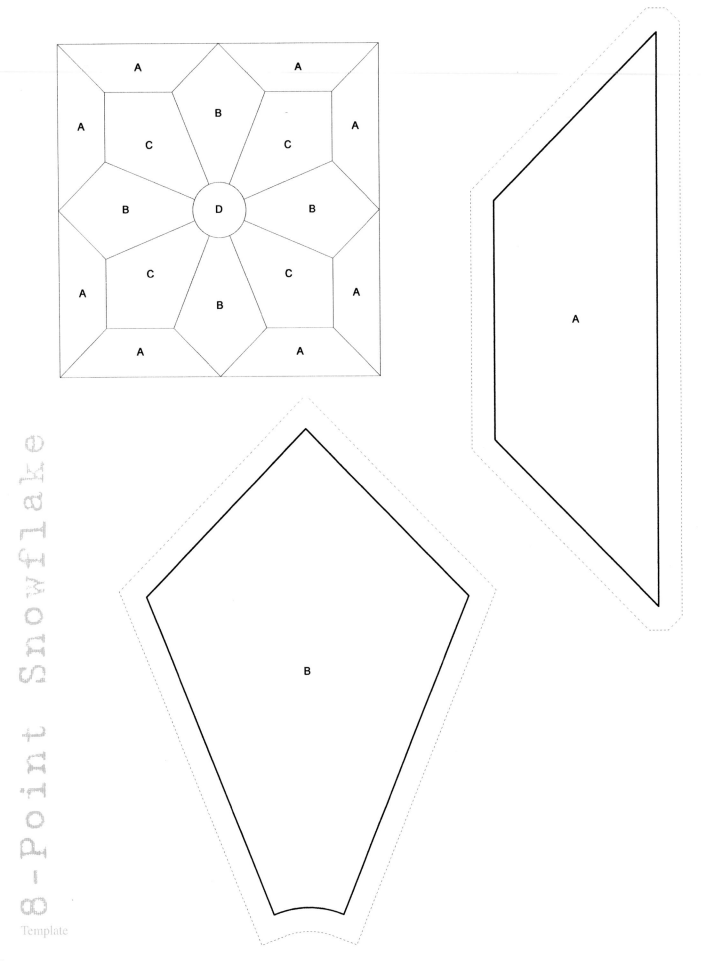

8-Point Snowflake

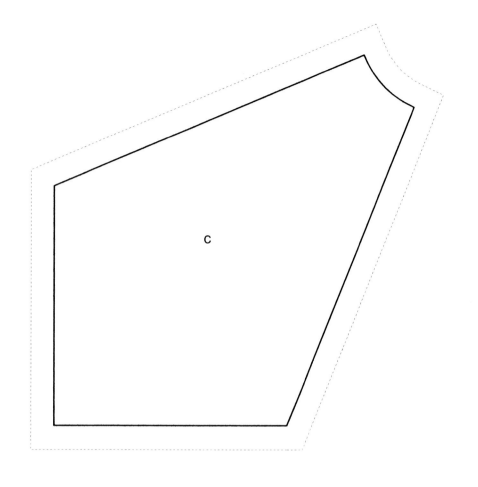

C

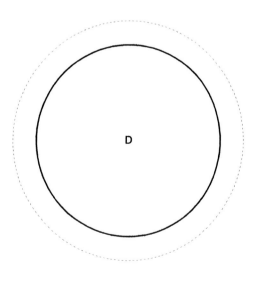

D

Template

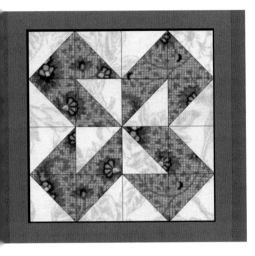

Colorado Quilt

Block Size: 12" finished

Appeared in The Star **January 8, 1941**

Fabric Needed:

Green print

Cream

This block is perfect for those who like to piece and cut without templates.

Cutting Directions

From the green print, cut

8 – 3 7/8" squares (if you prefer to use templates, cut 16 triangles using template A)

From the cream fabric, cut

8 – 3 7/8" squares (if you prefer to use templates, cut 16 triangles using template A)

To Make the Block

If you cut squares from the green print and cream fabrics, draw a line from corner to corner on the diagonal on the reverse side of the cream fabric. Place a cream square atop a green print square with right sides facing and sew 1/4" on either side of the line. Using your rotary cutter, cut on the line. Open each of the half-square triangle units and press toward the dark fabric.

If you chose to cut the triangles using template A, sew the green print and cream triangles together to make 16 half-square triangles.

Sew the half-square triangles into rows of four as shown below.

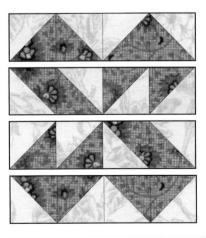

Colorado Quilt

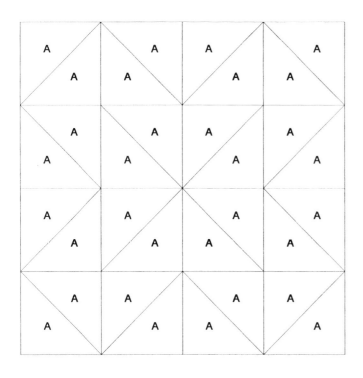

Colorado Quilt

From The Kansas City Star,

January 8, 1941:

No. 636

A Northwestern Kansas woman, Mrs. Pearl Bacon of Achilles, has given us this design as a friendly token to the state on Kansas's western boundary line. It is well adapted to sharp contrasts between very dark and light pieces. The creator of the pattern used unbleached muslin for her light blocks. Any light 1-tone material and prints would be attractive combinations.

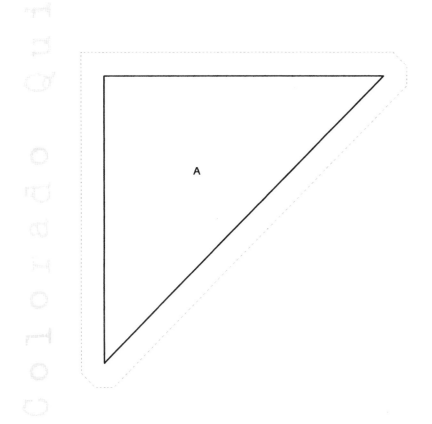

A

To Make the Block

Paper-piece the four A sections. The inner triangles will be red and the outer triangles will be blue.

Rising Sun

Block Size: 12" finished

Fabric Needed:

Red

Blue

Tan

Sew the red and blue C pieces together, alternating the colors.

For this challenging block, we will use a combination of paper-piecing and templates.

Cutting Directions

From the red fabric, cut

6 pieces using template C

1 circle using template D

24 triangles – measure one of the triangles on the paper-piecing template. Cut out a template that is 1/2-inch larger on all three sides. You will have plenty of allowance for your seams.

Press the seam allowance under the center circle and appliqué it to the center of the block.

From the blue fabric, cut

6 pieces using template C

28 triangles – measure one of the triangles on the paper-piecing template. Cut out a template that is 1/2-inch larger on all three sides. You will have plenty of allowance for your seams. Notice that the triangles on each end of the strip are smaller.

Fold the center of the block in half and lightly press a crease in the fold.

fold

From the tan fabric, cut

4 pieces using template B

Fold the block in half again and lightly press creases in the fold.

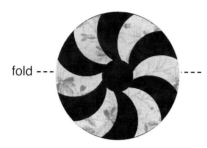

Sew the four A sections together leaving the last seam open.

Match up the seam allowances and the pressed creases. Pin in place. Pin the outer circle all the way around the inner circle being very careful to match where the seams intersect. Stitch together. Close up the last A seam.

Sew the four tan B pieces together, leaving the last seam open. Pin to the inside of the block, being careful to match the seam allowances. Sew in place and close up the last seam.

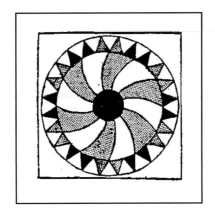

From The Kansas City Star, February 2, 1929:

No. 20

This is a quilt pattern for which many requests have been received. It is rather an intricate pattern, but will not daunt the quilter who aspires to a design that is both lovely and unusual. All the patterns given here are for one block. Make cardboard cutting patterns, and mark lightly around them onto material. Then cut a seam larger all around and sew back to the pencil lines. First piece four small triangles, two white and two in color, into a block which in turn is sewed to the curved block. When twelve of these are pieced sew the long seams which make it into a wheel. The "hub" is creased around and appliqued to center. This whole wheel, or sun, may either be appliqued on a 12-inch square, or pieced in with the four white corner blocks as shown in the pattern. Flame red and orange with white, unbleached or yellow muslin are appropriate for this pattern.

From The Kansas City Star, September 26, 1936:

No. 473

"The Rising Sun" is one of the early colonial patterns which is now revived by quilt fans. Choose your own colors and allow for seams. This design is sent by Mrs. Cecelia Becker, Owensville, Mo., an ardent quilt fan.

From The Kansas City Star, September 12, 1956:

No. 994

The Rising Sun, reputed to be one of the oldest patterns of American quiltmakers, was a pattern reproduced in Weekly Star Farmer years ago. Emma W. Survicegood, 723 South Indian avenue, Tulsa, Okla., sent it from her collection, thinking today's quiltmakers might be interested.

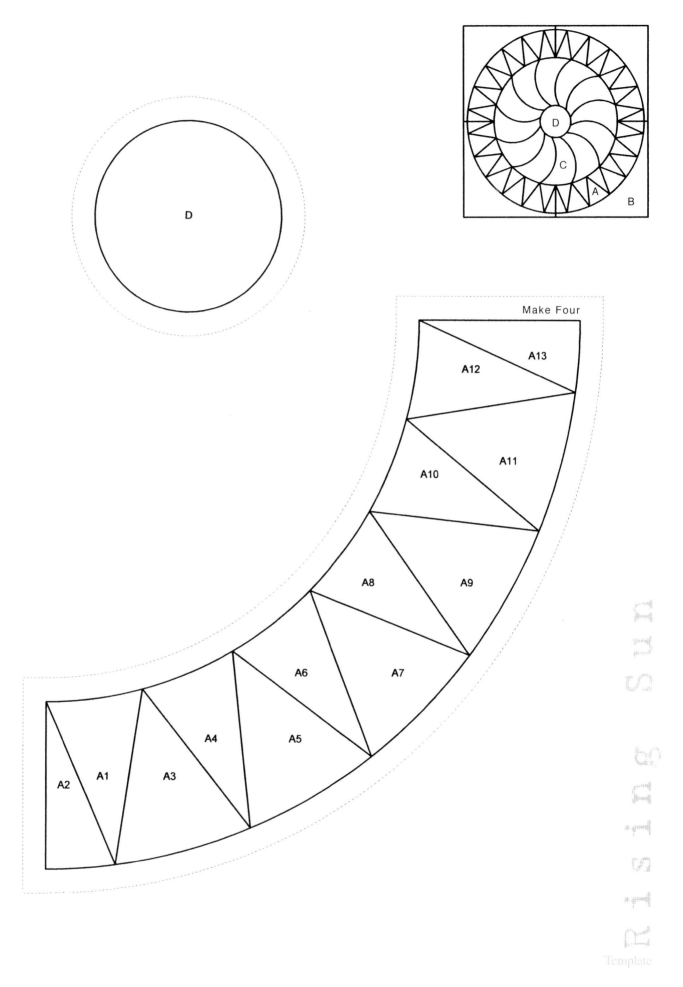

D

Make Four

A13
A12
A11
A10
A8
A9
A6
A7
A4
A5
A2
A1
A3

Rising Sun

Template

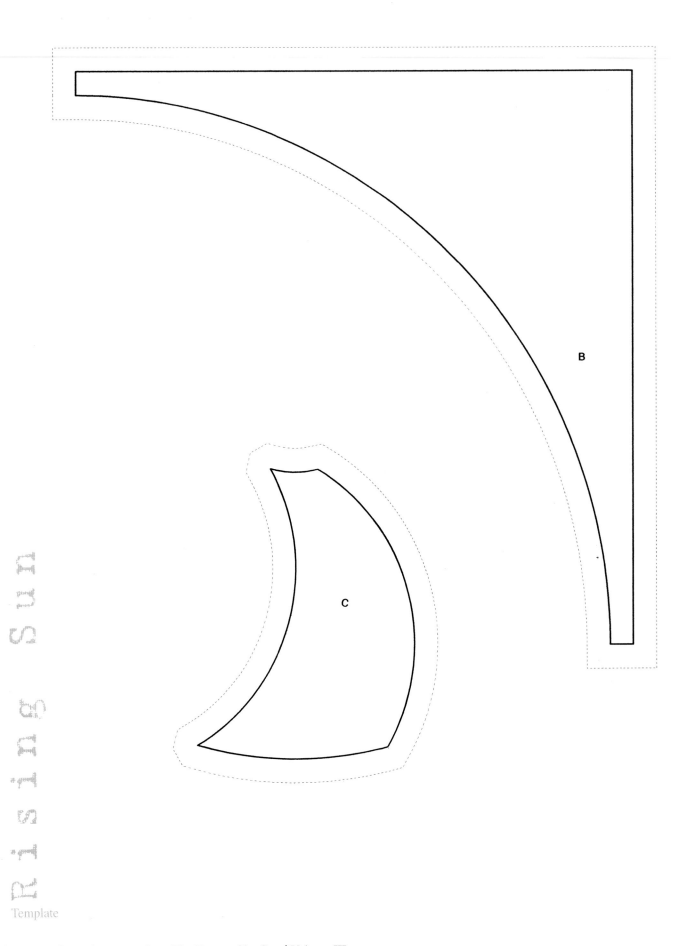

B

C

Rising Sun

Template

Rising Sun submitted by Sue Bouchard, Vista, Calif. Quiltmaker unknown. Owned by Sue Bouchard.

Arkansas Snowflake

Block Size: 6" finished

Fabric needed:

Background

Teal

Purple

Due to the odd shapes of the pieces, we will be giving template directions rather than rotary cutting instructions.

From the background fabric, cut

4 pieces using template A

From the teal fabric, cut

2 pieces using template B

From the purple fabric, cut

2 pieces using template B

Appeared in The Star **February 9, 1935**

To Make the Block

1 Sew a purple B piece to a teal B piece. Make two. Don't sew all the way to the end of the seams as they will be inset later.

2 Sew the two units together as shown. Don't sew all the way to the end of the seams as they will be inset later.

3 Inset the 4 background B pieces to complete the block.

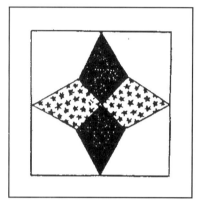

From The Kansas City Star,

February 9, 1935:

No. 388

This pattern, called the Arkansas Star or the Snow Flake, is one that a child can do. The completed quilt is lovely in print and plain blocks on white or pale lemon background. It was contributed by a quilt fan, Mrs. J. L. Wiesle, Brinkley, Ark.

History of the Block

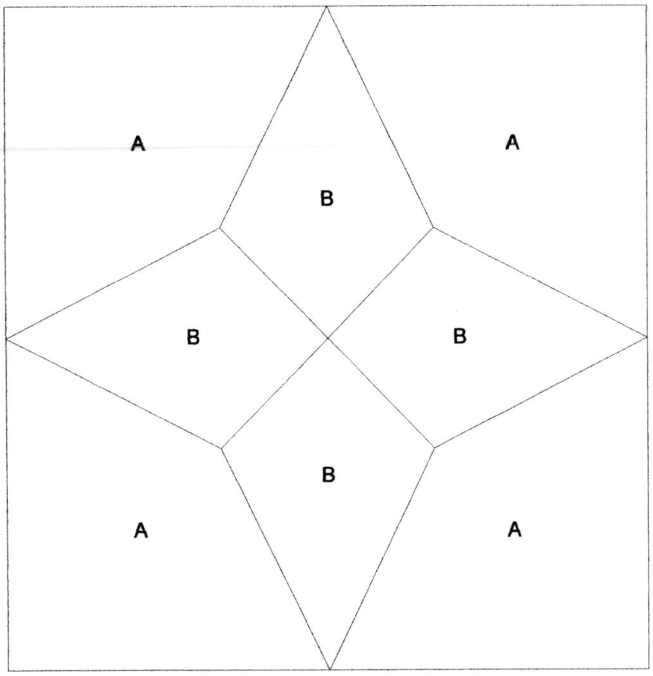

A   A

B

B   B

B

A   A

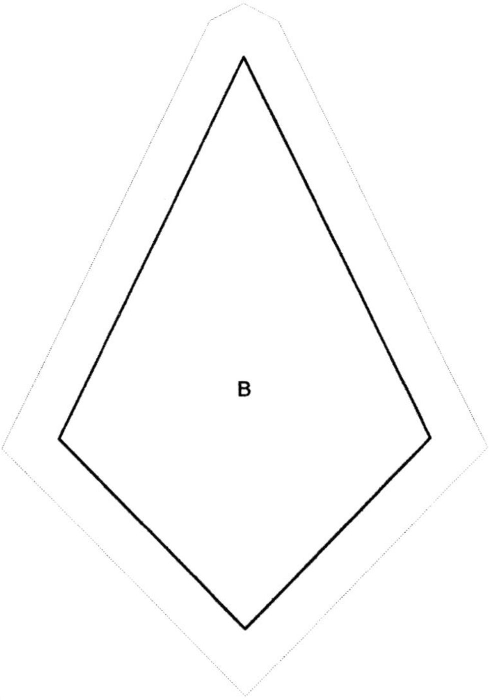

B

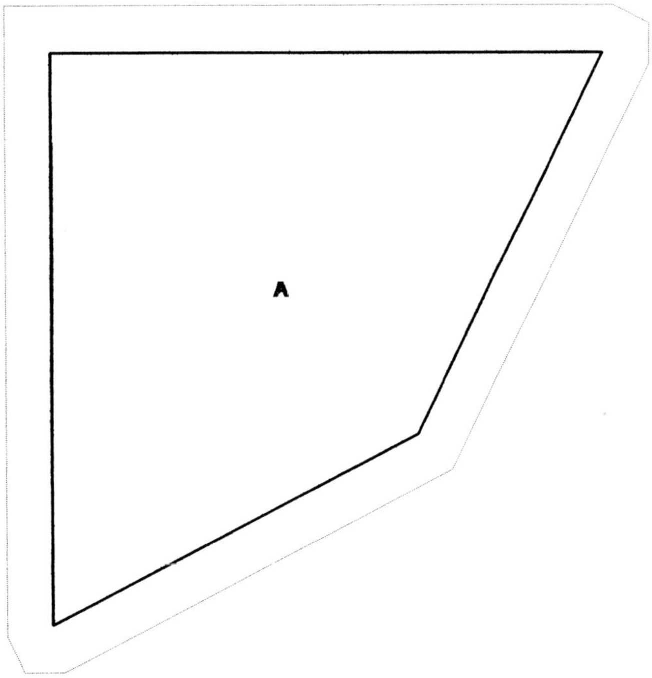

A

Template

16

Appeared in The Star **July 11, 1945**

Diversion Quilt

Block Size: 6" finished

To Make the Block

1 Make a mark 1/4" in from each corner on the reverse side of the square and on the reverse side of the shortest edges of the A pieces.

Pin the light brown pieces to the center square and stitch in place. Begin and end sewing at the 1/4" marks. NOTE: Do not sew past the 1/4" marks. If you do, your block will not lie flat and you can end up with little pleats in the corners.

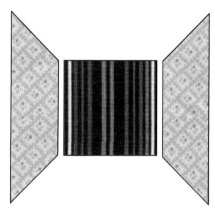

2 Now sew the dark brown A pieces in place. Again, sew exactly to the mark.

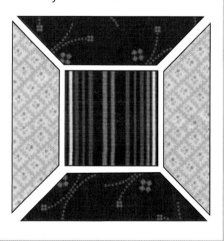

Fabric needed:

Brown stripe

Dark brown print

Light brown print

We will be using templates for this block.

From the brown striped fabric, cut

1 – 3 1/2" square (template B)

From the dark brown print fabric, cut

2 pieces using template A

From the light brown print fabric, cut

2 pieces using template A

Diversion Quilt

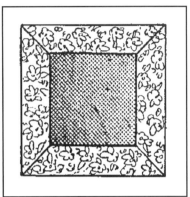

From The Kansas City Star,

July 11, 1945:

No. 769

Original size – 6"

Because it is so easy to make, Miss Bonnie Maze, Star route, Hugo, Colo., has named this the Diversion quilt. In her specimen block both the center square and border were of print. Another pleasing combination would be a 1-tone center surrounded with prints, or a reversal of this order.

Remove the block from under the presser foot of your machine, then pin the mitered corners together. Begin sewing 1 or 2 threads away from the marks and stitch all corners toward the outside edge of the block.

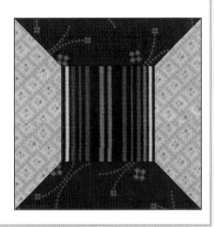

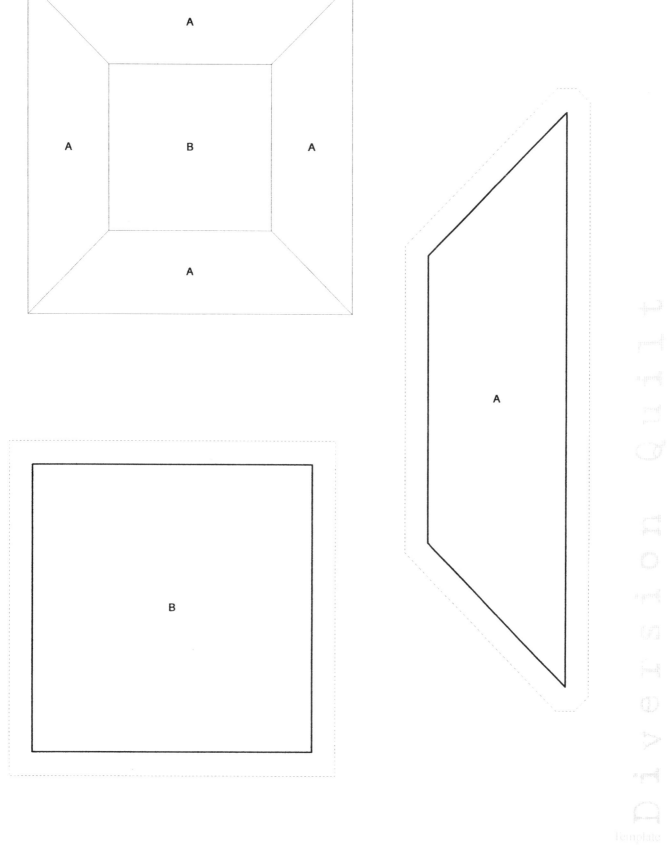

Wagon Wheel
Block Size: 12" finished

Fabric Needed
Cheddar
Red
Brown
Beige

This difficult block is much easier if it is paper pieced. I recommend you cut all your pieces 1/2" larger than needed all the way around each piece. I've also found I like Carol Doak's Paper for this method better than anything else I've tried. Another hint: Use double-sided sticky tape to hold your fabric in place. The tape tends to stick to the paper rather than the fabric when it comes time to remove the paper. This works especially well with pieces F1 and G1 since you just need to hold them in place until you stitch them to the E pieces.

If you are going to paper piece a quilt, let me remind you to leave the paper on until the entire top is sewn together.

Cutting Instructions
From the red, cut
40 triangles total for the A and B units
16 triangles total for the E units
4 wedges for the center circle

From the brown fabric, cut
4 rectangles for position C1
4 triangles for position D1

From the beige fabric, cut
4 pieces for position G1

From the cheddar fabric, cut
40 triangles total for the A and B units
20 triangles total for the E units
4 wedges for position F1
4 wedges for the center circle

Sew the pieces to the paper in the order given on each template. You will need to print out and make 4 of each unit until you get to the center circle. You will need to make 1 each of those two units.

Red fabric is used in the following positions:
A2 – A3 – A5 – A7 – A9
B2 – B3 – B5 – B7 – B9
E1 – E4 – E6 – E8
H1 – H3
I1 – I3

The cheddar fabric is used in the following positions:
A1 – A4 – A6 – A8 – A10
B1 – B4 – B6 – B8 – B10
E2 – E3 – E5 – E7 – E9
F1
H2 – H4
I2 – I4

The beige fabric is used in the following position:
G1

The brown fabric is used in the following positions:
C1
D1

Print out 4 copies of each unit except for the center triangle. You only need one copy of that.

Wagon Wheel

To Make the Block

Stitch the red and cheddar triangles in place on unit A and B.

Sew unit A to unit C. Then add unit B. Add unit D1. Make 4.

Sew the red and cheddar triangles in place on unit E.

Add a cheddar F1 unit and a beige G1 as shown. Make 4.

Sew an F-E-G unit to either side of an A-C-B-D unit as shown. You need to make two of these.

Now add the two remaining A-C-B-D units. Leave one seam open.

Stitch the unit H and the unit I wedges together.

From The Kansas City Star,

June 23, 1934:

No. 359

For several weeks this department has been petting the quilt makers who were beginners by giving them easy patterns. This week the pattern is for experts, none others need try it. Cut every piece true. Begin at the center, piece the circle, then the four spokes with the triangles, then the quarter circles between. Good luck to you.

Pin the center circle in place and stitch.

Close up the last seam to complete the block.

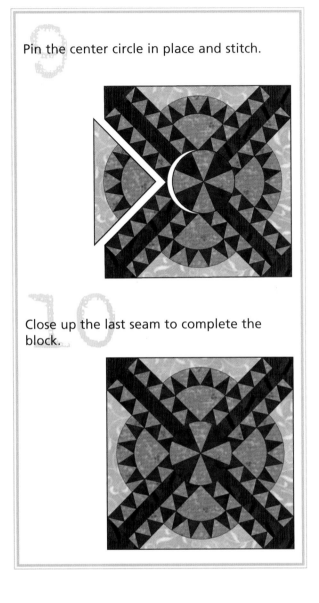

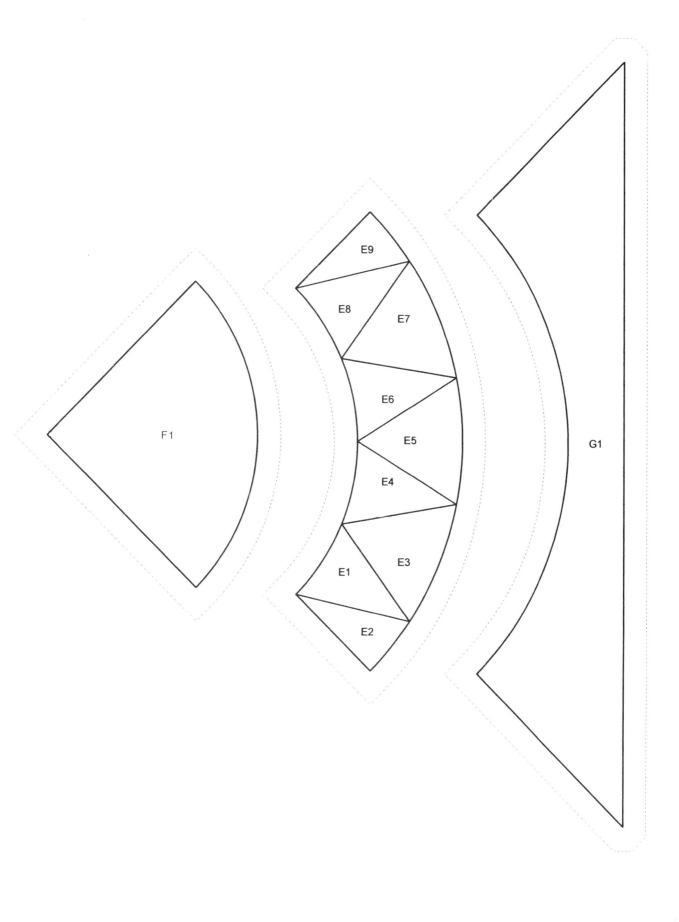

E9

E8

E7

E6

E5

E4

E3

E1

E2

F1

G1

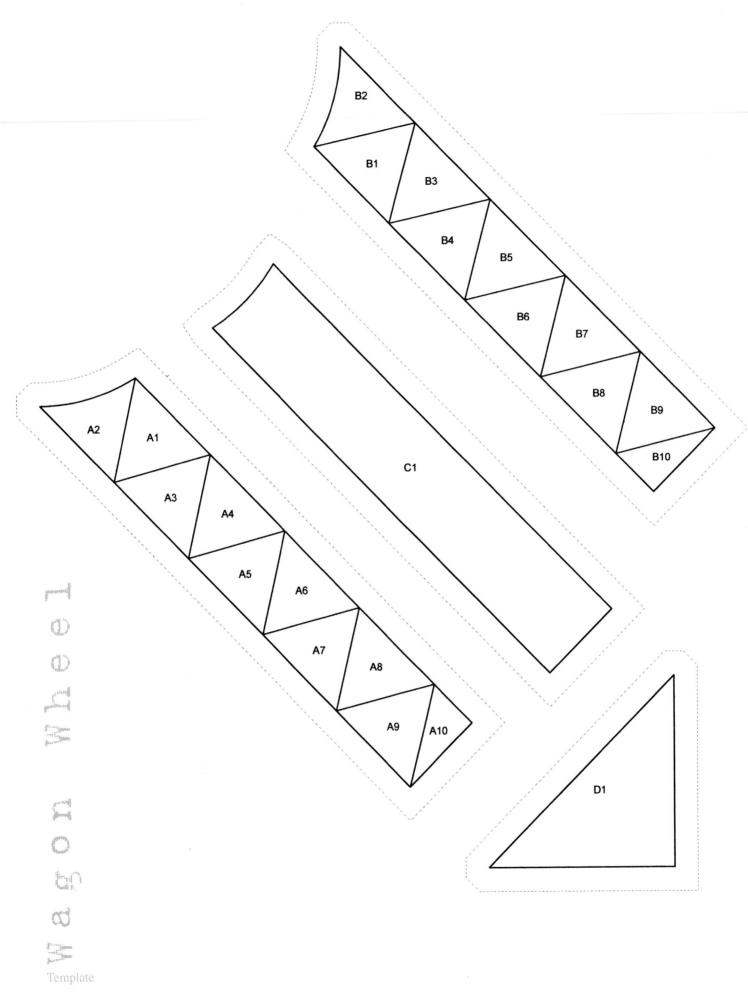

B2

B1

B3

B4

B5

B6

B7

B8

B9

B10

A2

A1

A3

A4

A5

A6

A7

A8

A9

A10

C1

D1

Wagon Wheel

Template

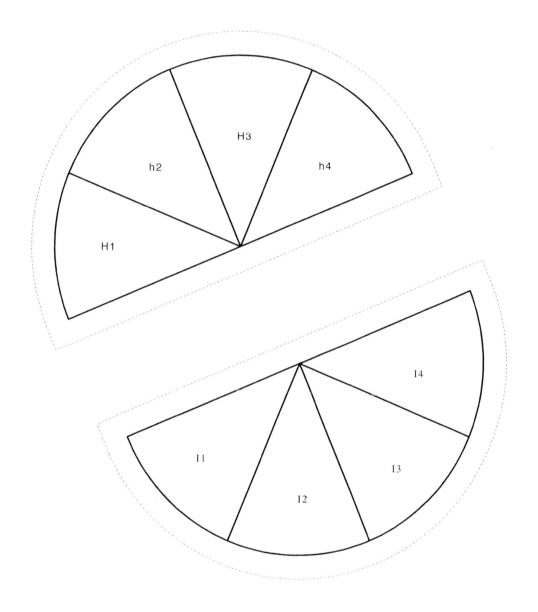

Return of the Swallows

Block Size: 12" finished

Fabric Needed

Dark blue

Medium blue

Cream

You can easily rotary cut the pieces for this block.

Cutting Directions

From the dark blue, cut

1 – 7 1/4" square or 4 triangles using template A. Cut the square from corner to corner twice on the diagonal

From the medium blue, cut

1 – 7 1/4" square or 4 triangles using template A. Cut the square from corner to corner twice on the diagonal

From the cream fabric, cut

8 – 3 7/8" squares or 16 B triangles. Cut the squares from corner to corner once on the diagonal.

To Make the Block

Sew two of the cream B triangles to a medium blue A triangle. Make 4.

Sew the remaining cream B triangles to the dark blue A triangles. Make 4.

Sew the flying geese together as shown. Notice the change in position where you stitch the dark blue flying geese.

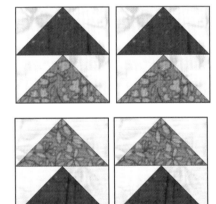

Sew the units together as shown to complete the block.

Return of the Swallows

From The Kansas City Star,

October 2, 1946:

No. 796

This is one of the popular quilt blocks designed by Mrs. A. B. Snyder, Flats, Neb. All the triangular pieces are the same. The center of the quilt is the square of triangles. Increase in size is achieved by adding strips of plain and print triangles with white strips of material set between.

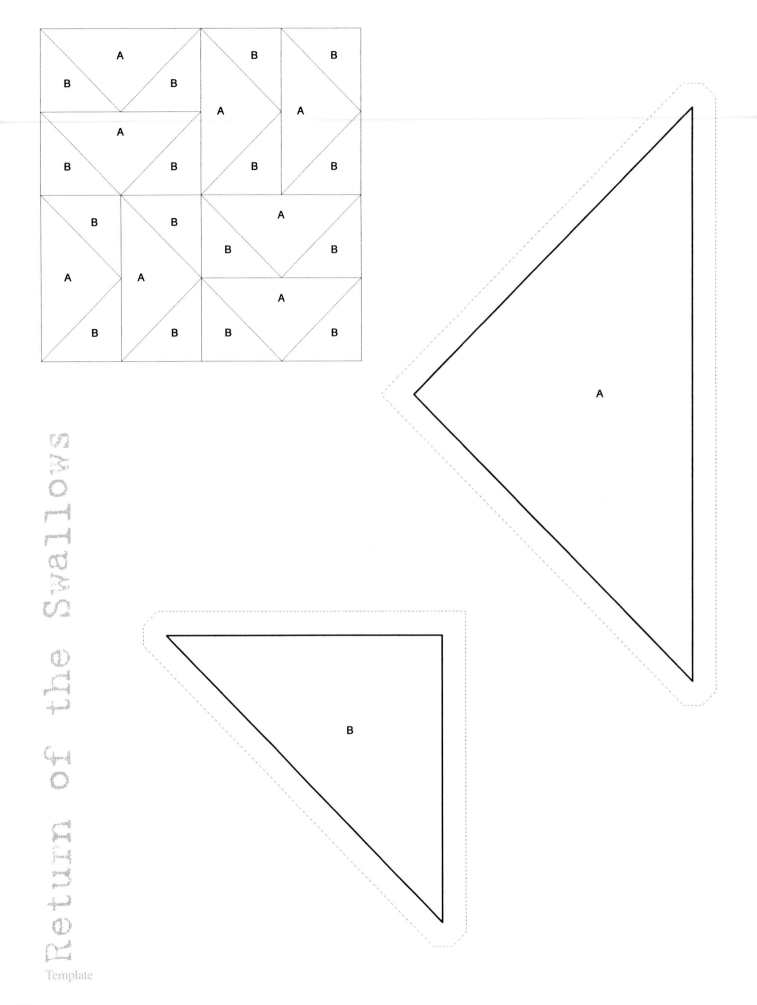

Return of the Swallows

Template

Pretty Pansy Posey Patch by Lynda Hall, Apopka, FL. Designed and quilted by Lynda Hall.

To Make the Block

Sew the light orange E triangles to the blue E triangles thus making 4 half-square triangles. Set these aside for the moment.

Sew the center of the block together by pairing piece H to piece J. You need to make 4 pairs as shown.

Make one-half of the center of the block by sewing two pairs together. Sew the two halves together.

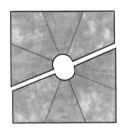

Baste the center circle in place to stabilize the block. You'll want to actually appliqué that piece in place last.

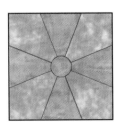

Hearts Desire
Block Size: 12" finished

Fabric Needed
Blue
Medium orange
Light orange

Because of the oddly shaped pieces and measurements, we will be using templates for this block. Also, I decided to add a seam to make this easier to piece.

Cutting Directions
From the medium orange, cut
4 pieces using template J
4 triangles using template G
4 pieces using template F
4 pieces using template I
1 circle using template K

From the light orange, cut
20 triangles using template E
8 rectangles using template D
8 squares using template A

From the blue, cut
4 squares using template A
4 triangles using template E
4 triangles using template B
4 triangles using template C
4 triangles using template H

To make the outer part of the block, sew an E triangle to each side of triangle G. Add a D rectangle. Make 4.

Sew a blue C triangle to an orange I triangle. Now add a light orange E triangle.

Sew the orange F triangle to the blue B triangle. Add a light E triangle. Sew the two pieces together. Make 4.

Sew the two rows together as shown.

Now make 4-patch units by sewing a light orange A square to the blue/light orange half-square triangle.

Sew a blue A square to a light orange A square. Sew the four squares together. Make 4.

Sew the block together in rows as shown.

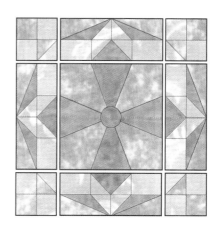

From The Kansas City Star,

January 16, 1932:

No. 212

Many a simple pattern has been shown for the quiltmaker who is not an expert. This is for the woman who can make the most difficult pattern. Allow for seams, be careful when cutting the patterns. Patience and skill are required, otherwise leave this quilt to those who have both.

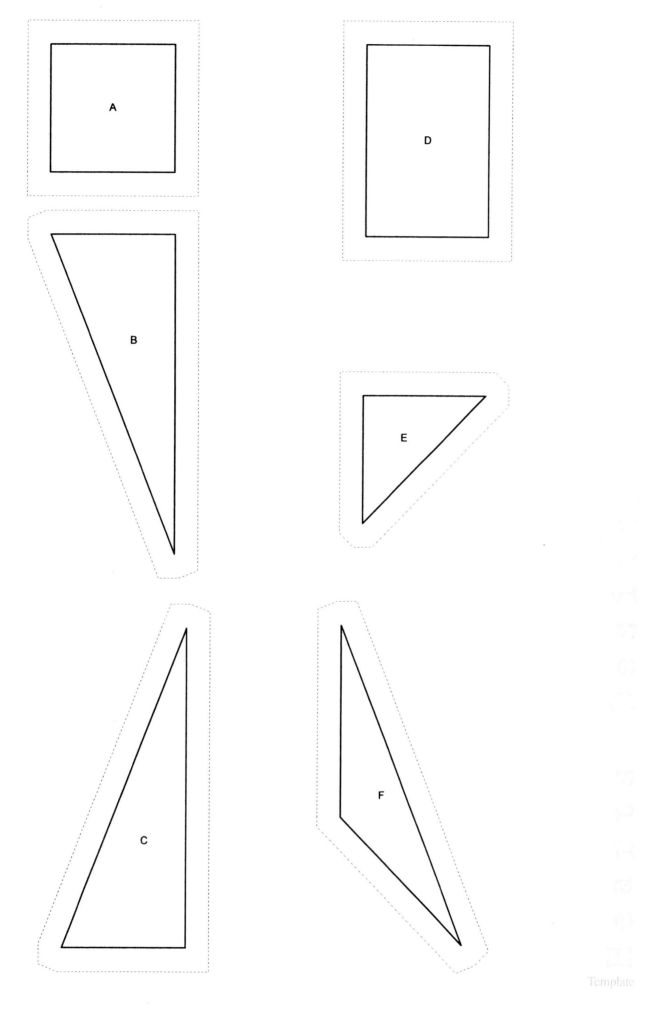

G

H

J

I

K

Template

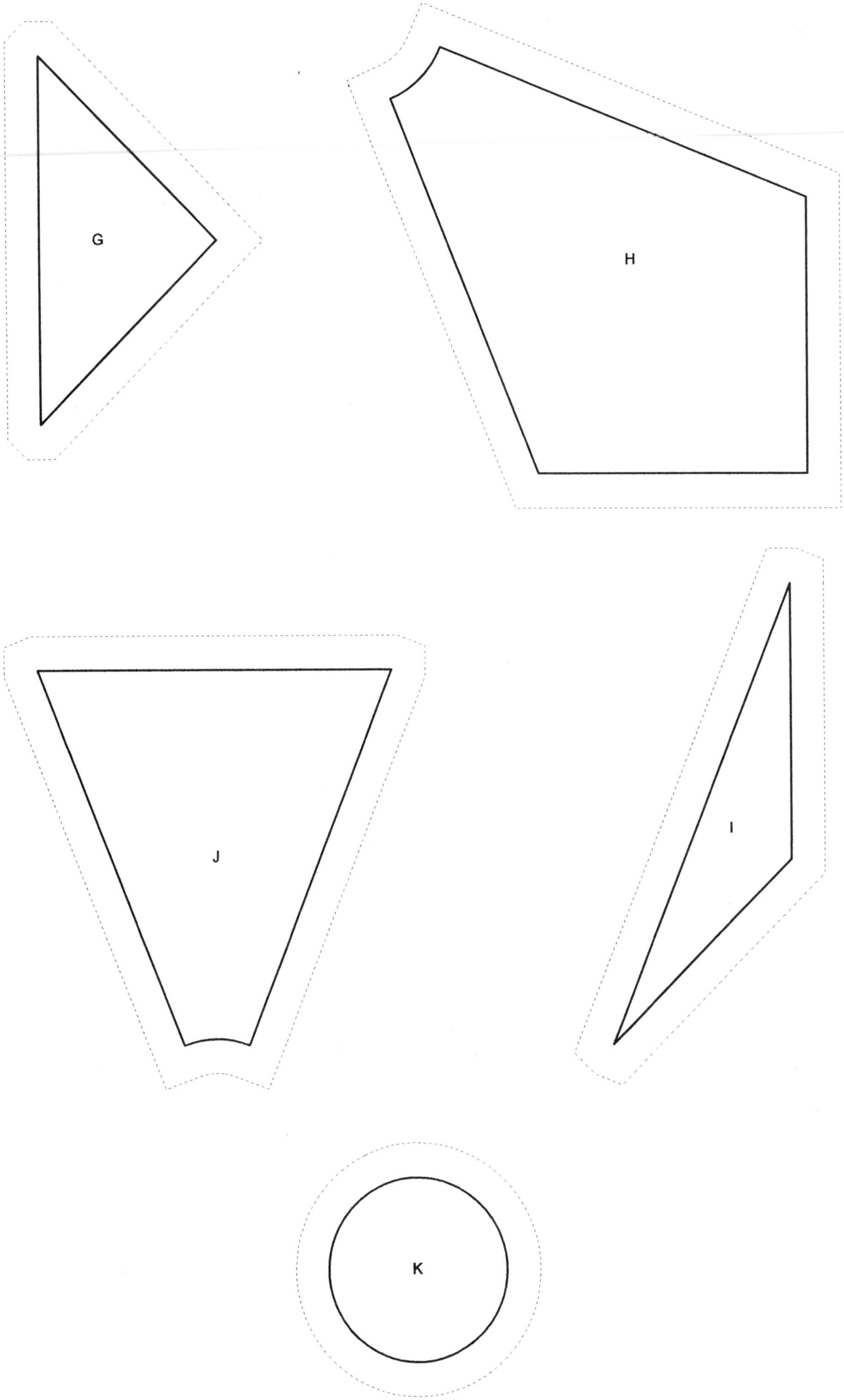

Appeared in The Star **September 9, 1959**

Fabric Needed

Red

Tan

To Make the Block

Sew the pieces to the paper in the order printed on each pattern. You'll need to print out and make 4 A units and 4 B units.

Sew the A units to the B units along the diagonal. Each AB unit comprises one-fourth of the block.

Sew the four AB units together to complete the block. Don't forget to wait until all your blocks are sewn together into a completed top before you remove the paper.

Here's a block that is far easier to make when paper pieced. I recommend you cut all your pieces 1/2" larger than needed all the way around each piece. I've also found I like Carol Doak's paper for this method better than anything else I've tried. Another hint: Use double-sided sticky tape to hold your fabric in place. The tape tends to stick to the paper rather than the fabric when it comes time to remove the paper.

If you are going to paper piece a quilt, let me remind you to leave the paper on until the entire top is sewn together.

From the red, cut the pieces for the following positions:

A1 – A3 – A5

B1 – B3 – B5

From the tan, cut the pieces for the following positions:

A2 – A4

B2 – B4

Carnival Time

From The Kansas City Star,

September 9, 1959:

No. 1036

This fascinating block may be developed in a wide variety of color teaming. The outer circle would be particularly engaging in two alternating, red and blue, for instance, with the inner circle cut from one of those colors. It is suggested that the prints be of small design. The contributor of the design is Mrs. May Bess, route 1, box 78, Poplar Bluff, Mo.

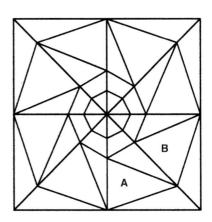

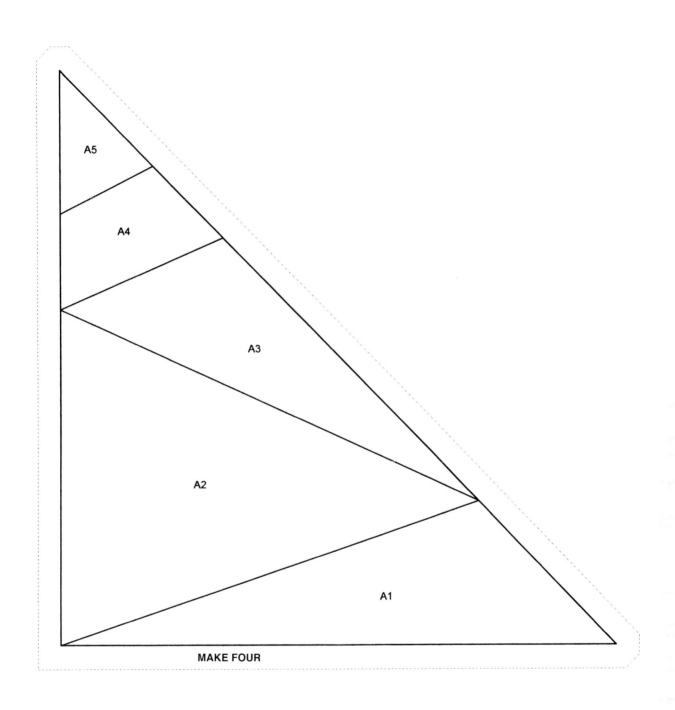

A5

A4

A3

A2

A1

MAKE FOUR

MAKE FOUR

B5

B4

B3

B2

B1

Carnival time

Template

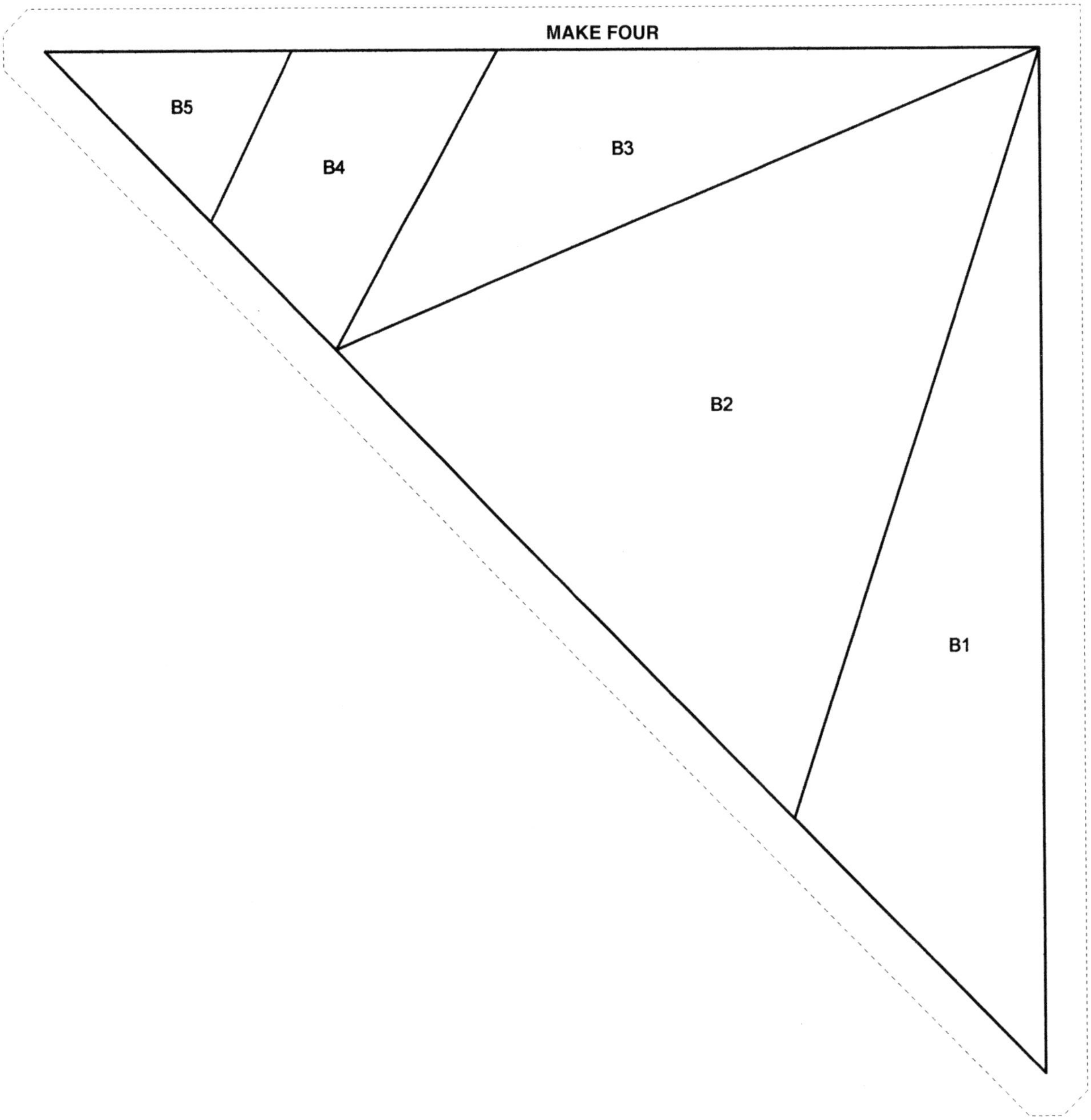

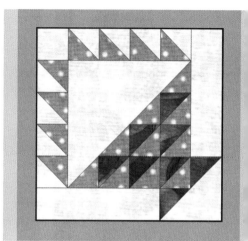

Appeared in The Star **December 16, 1942**

Basket Quilt in Triangles
Block Size: 12" finished

To Make the Block

To make half-square triangles, draw a line from corner to corner on the reverse side of the lightest fabric. Place the cream colored squares atop the blue print squares. Sew 1/4" on either side of the line. Cut along the line with your rotary cutter, open each half-square triangle unit and press toward the darker fabric. You need 8 blue print/cream half-square triangles.

Fabric Needed
Cream
Blue print
Medium blue

Follow the above instructions and make 6 medium blue and blue print half-square triangles.

You'll be happy to know that you can use your rotary cutter for this block instead of templates!

Cutting Directions
From the cream fabric, cut
1 – 2 1/2" square or use template A
4 – 2 7/8" squares or
8 triangles using template B
1 – 8 7/8" square cut once on the diagonal
(This is piece E and no template is given.)
1 – 4 7/8" square cut once on the diagonal
or use template D
2 – 8 1/2" x 2 1/2" rectangles or use template C

For the handle portion of the basket, sew 4 half-square triangles together into a strip as shown. Sew the strip to the side of triangle E.

From the medium blue, cut
4 – 2 7/8" squares. Cut one square once on the diagonal and we'll use the 3 remaining squares for half-square triangles.

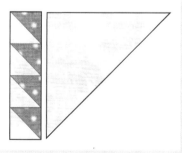

From the blue print, cut
9 – 2 7/8" squares. Cut two squares once on the diagonal and we'll use the 7 remaining squares for half-square triangles.

Basket Quilt in Triangles

Now sew another strip of 4 half-square tri-angles together. Stitch the A square on the left hand side of the strip. Then sew the strip to the E triangle as shown.

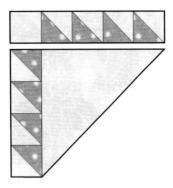

To make the body of the basket, sew the blue print triangle and the blue print/medi-um blue half-square triangles into rows as shown. Then sew the rows together.

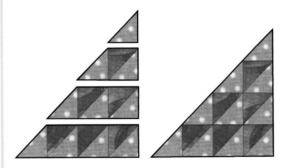

Join the top part of the basket to the bot-tom of the basket. Your block should now look like this.

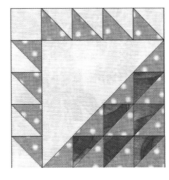

Sew a medium blue triangle to the C rec-tangles as shown. Be careful of the direc-tion of the triangle. One must mirror image the other.

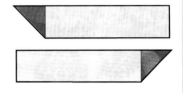

Sew the rectangles to two sides of the basket as shown.

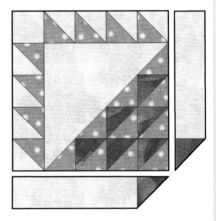

Sew the cream D triangle in place to complete the block.

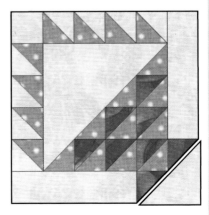

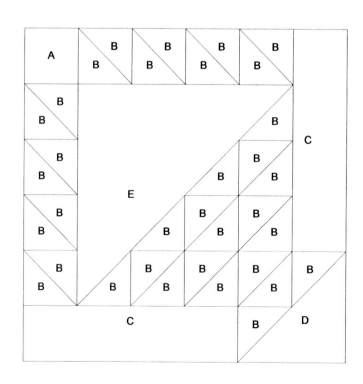

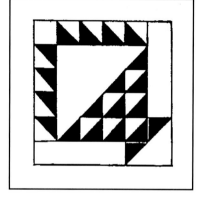

From The Kansas City Star,

December 16, 1942:

No.706

Unbleached muslin and solid bright red were the colors originally used for the triangles of this basket motif block, copied from an old quilt by Mrs. Myrtle Schwerdt, R. R. 4, Warrenton, Mo.

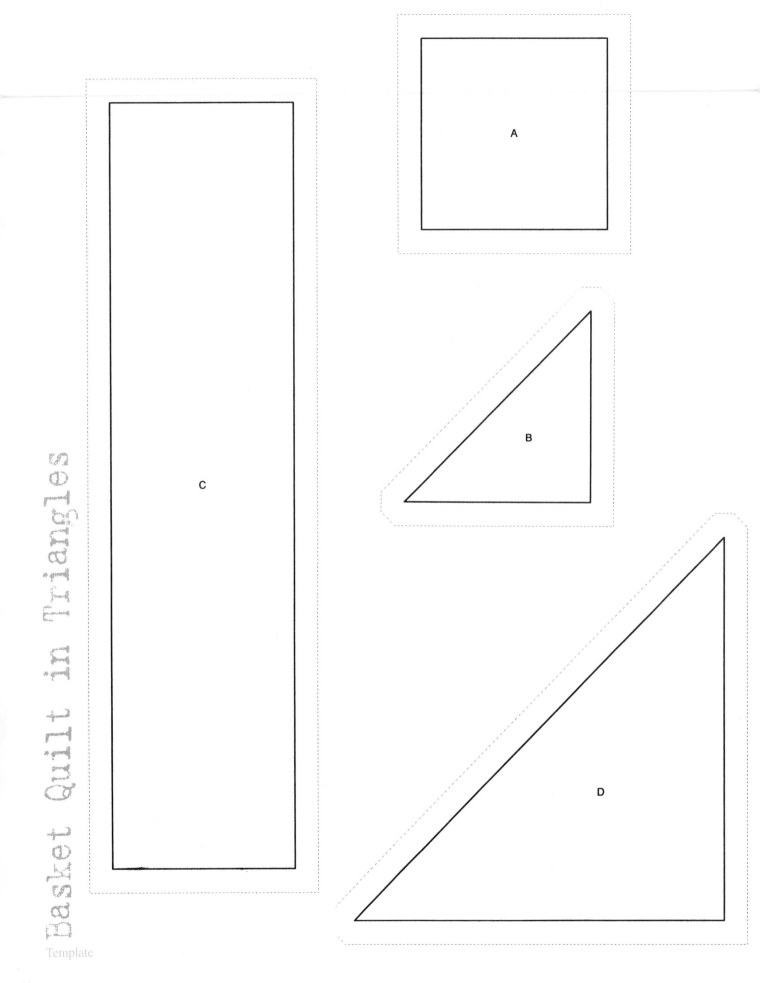

A

B

C

D

Basket Quilt in Triangles

Template

Appeared in The Star **March 6, 1937**

To Make the Block

Draw a line from corner to corner on the diagonal on the reverse side of the medium blue squares. Place each medium blue square atop a dark blue square and sew 1/4" on either side of the line. Using your rotary cutter, cut on the line. Open each unit and press toward the darkest fabric. You should have 4 large half-square triangles and 28 small half-square triangles. If you cut triangles, sew each together along the diagonal to make half-square triangles.

Sew 3 small half-square triangles into a strip. Make four strips.

Sew a strip to one side of the large half-square triangle. Make four.

Sew the remaining small half-square triangles into four rows of four.

Waves of the Sea

Block Size: 12" finished

Fabric needed:

Medium blue

Dark blue

Cutting Directions

From the dark blue, cut

2 – 5 3/8" squares or

4 triangles using template B

14 – 2 3/8" squares or

28 triangles using template B

From the medium blue, cut

2 – 5 3/8" squares

or 4 triangles using template B

14 – 2 3/8" squares

or 28 triangles using template B

Waves of the Sea

From The Kansas City Star,

March 6, 1937:

No. 493

Here is a quilt that can be made quickly in any colors desired. Allow for seams. This design is an old one contributed to The Star's quilt fans by Lora Stevens, Springfield, Mo. Thank you very much.

Sew a strip of four onto each unit you've made so far. You should have four units that look like this.

Sew the units together as shown to complete the block.

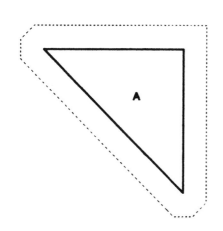

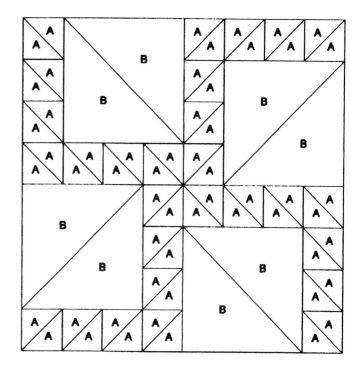

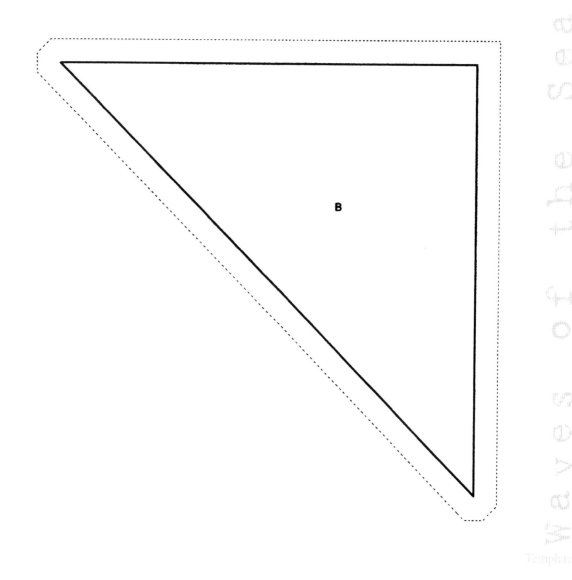

Thorny Thicket

Block Size: 12" finished

Fabric needed:

Tan

Olive green

Dark olive green

Due to the odd measurement of the pieces for a 12" block, we will be giving directions for template use.

From the tan fabric, cut

8 squares using template D

4 triangles using template A

4 triangles using template C

16 triangles using template B

From the olive green, cut

16 triangles using template B

From the dark olive green, cut

8 squares using template D

4 triangles using template E

To Make the Block

1 Alternating the tan and dark olive green squares, sew them together into strips of four. Make four rows and sew the rows together to make the center of the block as shown.

2 Sew the tan and olive green triangles together. Stitch the triangles together into strips of four. You'll need to make four sections like this for the outer part of the block.

3 Now make the four corner units by sewing a tan A and C triangle to the dark green E triangle. Make four.

4 Sew a corner unit to either end of an outer strip as shown. Make two.

5 Sew an outer strip to either side of the center square.

6 Sew the three sections together to complete the block.

From The Kansas City Star, August 5, 1942:
No. 695

The much desired "Thorny Thicket" is supplied by Mrs. Mae Dees, Coldwater, Mo., who found it among a pattern collection made during her childhood. She says when the youngsters of her day were learning to piece quilts they were first required to use their small scraps in this pattern before they were permitted to have large new pieces. Sometimes each thorn would be of a different color. Mrs. Dees suggests a color scheme of red, white and blue. The completed blocks are put together with blue strips 1 inch wide, having a white strip of the same width between them, and a red and white 9-patch in the corners.

History of the Block

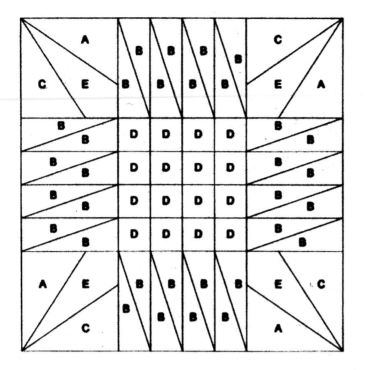

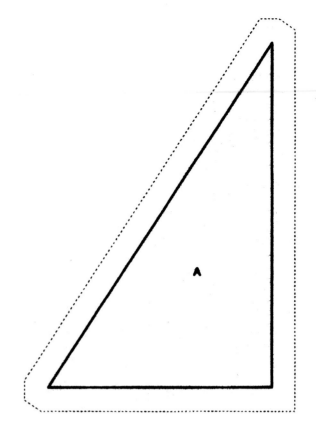

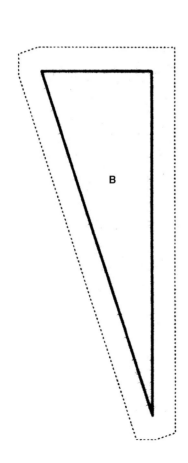

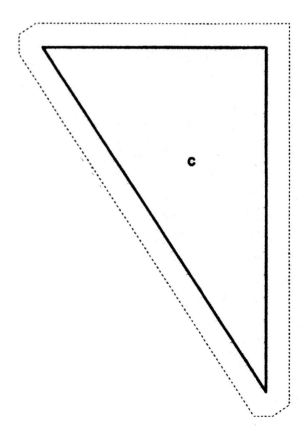

Thorny Thicket

Template

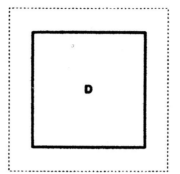

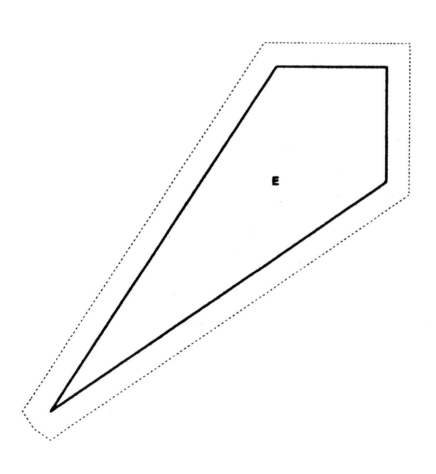

Roman Stripe

Block Size: 18" finished

Fabric Needed

3 shades of green –

light, medium and dark

1 dark red

1 tan check

1 light tan print

Here's a perfect pattern for those of you who have been buying jelly rolls

Cut 2 1/2" strips across the width of each piece of fabric. Sew the strips into groups of three strip sets.

Set 1 – light green/dark red/dark green

Set 2 – tan check/dark red/tan check

Set 3 – tan print/dark red/tan print

Set 4 – light green/dark red/medium green

Cut each strip set into 6 1/2" increments.

Appeared in The Star **December 21, 1955**

To Make the Block

Sew the sets into rows of three as shown.

From The Kansas City Star,

December 21, 1955:

No. 970

A rotation of three 1-tone pieces or a 3-part plan of small prints would be appropriate for the Roman Stripe. The design comes from Bennie Bess, route 1, box 78, Poplar Bluff, Mo.

Roman Stripe

Template

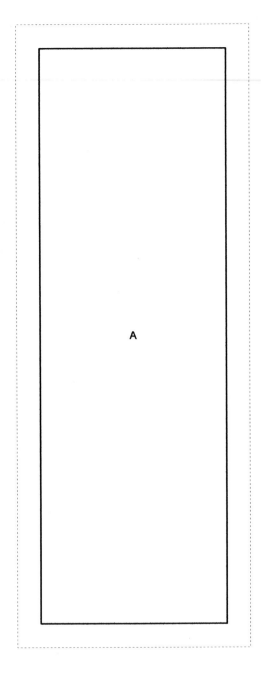

Split Rail by Jeanne Whaley, Stuart, FL. Design by M'Lis Rae Hawley from her book "Fat Quarter Quilts."
Sewed and quilted by Jeanne Whaley.

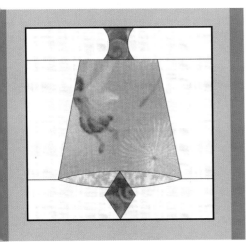

Bell

Block Size: 6" finished

Fabric Needed:

Light blue

Light medium blue

Medium blue

Dark medium blue

Due to the odd shapes in this pattern, we will be using templates.

Cutting directions:

From the light blue, cut

2 pieces using template A

1 piece using template C, D, E and F

From the dark medium blue, cut

1 piece using template B

1 piece using template J

From the medium blue, cut

1 piece using template G

From the light medium blue, cut

1 piece using template H

1 piece using template I

To Make the Block

Sew a light blue A piece to each side of the B piece.

Sew the light blue F piece and the light blue C piece to piece G.

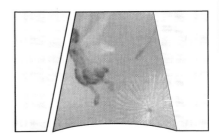

Sew piece H to E and I to D as shown.

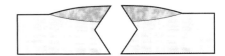

Stitch to either side of J.

Sew the three rows together to complete the block.

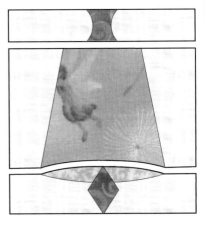

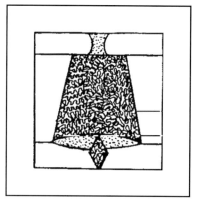

From The Kansas City Star,

March 15, 1961:

No. 1058

Listening to the tone of the bells on the cows as they came home late in the afternoon from grazing on the open range inspired the mother of Mrs. Mae Dees, route 1, Coldwater, Mo., to design this bell for a quilt block. Mrs. Dees says the pattern was designed at least 60 years ago. She recently found the tattered paper on which it was drawn, reconstructed it and mailed it to Weekly Star Farmer. It immediately impresses one as appropriate for members of any of the CowBelle organizations. Depending upon the metal chosen by a state group, the bell may be developed in copper or silver tones. A small print is suggested for the bell. The clapper is appliqued.

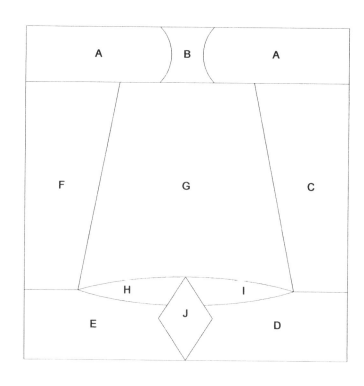

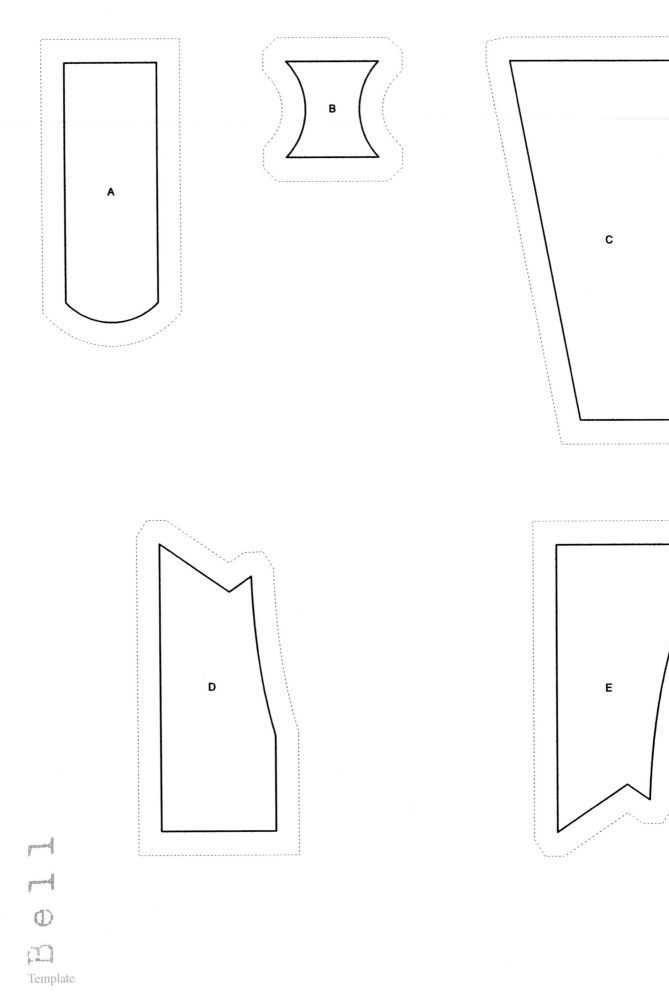

Template

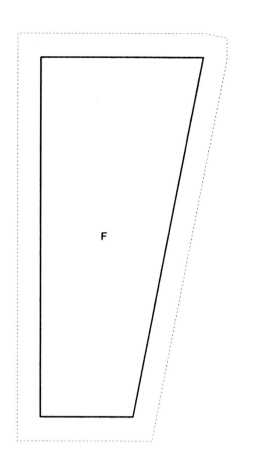

F

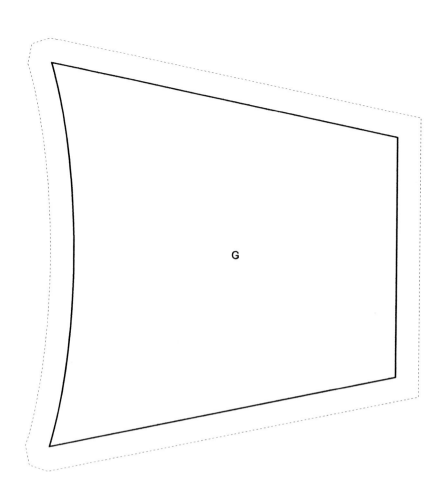

G

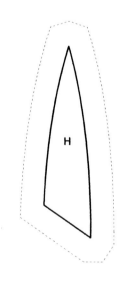

H

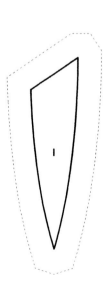

I

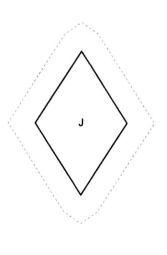

J

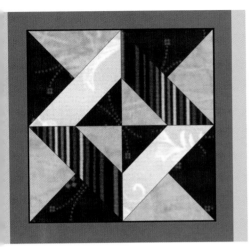

Four-Corner Puzzle

Block Size: 12" finished

Fabric needed:

Brown stripe

Light peach

Dark peach

Dark brown

Four-Corner Puzzle

We can combine rotary cutting instructions and templates for this pattern.

From the dark brown fabric, cut

1 – 7 1/4" square. Cut the square from corner to corner twice on the diagonal or cut 4 triangles using template A.

1 - 3 7/8" square. Cut the square from corner to corner once on the diagonal or cut 2 triangles using template C.

From the dark peach fabric, cut

1 – 7 1/4" square. Cut the square from corner to corner twice on the diagonal or cut 4 triangles using template A.

1 - 3 7/8" square. Cut the square from corner to corner once on the diagonal or cut 2 triangles using template C.

To Make the Block

Sew the dark brown and dark peach A triangles together. Make 4.

Sew a striped B piece to a dark peach C triangle. Make 2.

Stitch a light peach B piece to a dark brown C triangle. Make 2.

Add a dark brown/dark peach unit to each B/C unit as shown.

Sew the units together to complete the block.

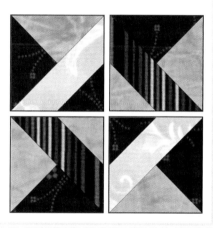

From The Kansas City Star,

July 21, 1943

No. 723

Original size – 6"

This pattern was copied by Miss Olive Boothe, Grand Pass, Mo., from a 75-year-old quilt.

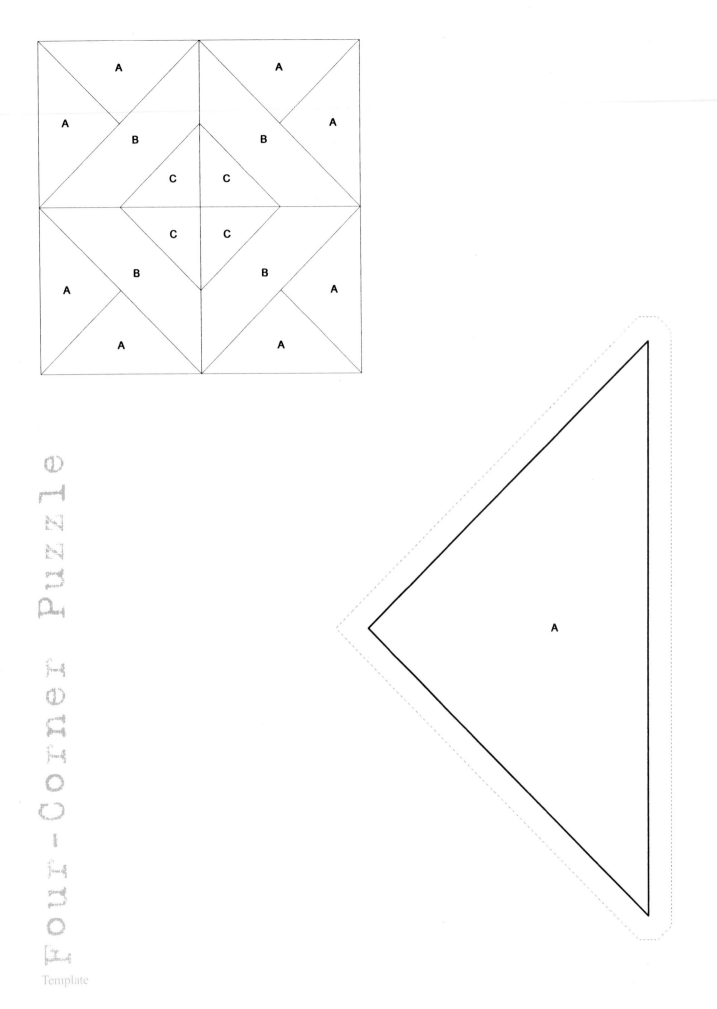

Four-Corner Puzzle

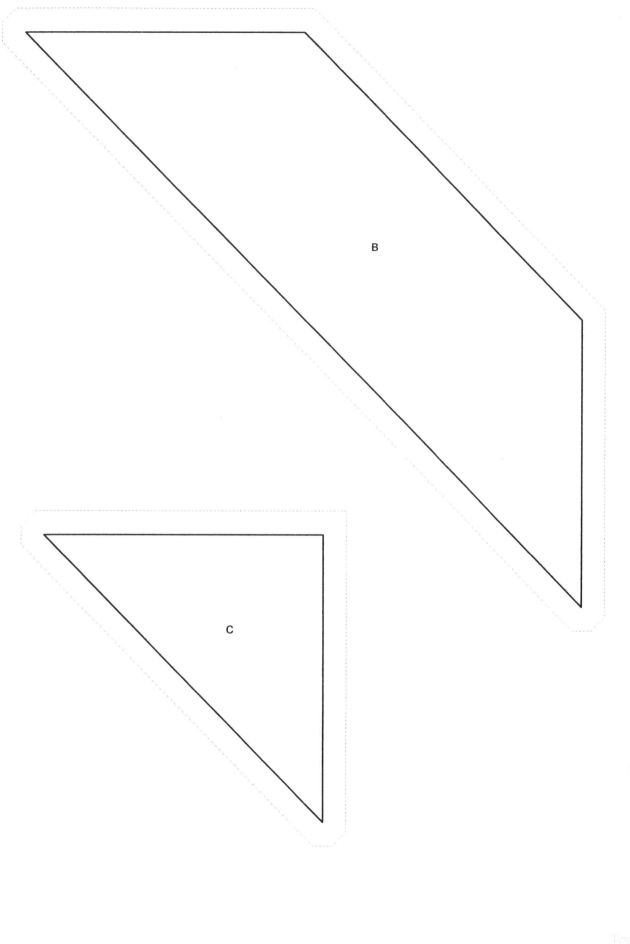

B

C

Four-Corner Puzzle

Template

Sun Rays

Block Size: 12" finished

Fabric Needed:
Yellow
Blue

We'll combine rotary cutting instructions along with templates.

NOTE: If you enjoy making this type of block, you might want to check out the Tri-Recs ruler set designed by Darlene Zimmerman and Joy Hoffman. It's made by EZ Quilting and is handier than a pocket on a shirt for making this type of block.

Cutting Directions
From the blue fabric, cut
5 – 4 1/2" squares (template A)
4 triangles using template B

From the yellow fabric, cut
4 triangles using template C
4 triangles using template D

To Make the Block

1. Sew a yellow C triangle and a yellow D triangle to a blue B triangle. Make four.

2. Sew an A square to either side of a triangle unit. Make two.

3. Sew a triangle unit to either side of a blue square as shown. Make one.

4. Sew the three rows together as shown to complete the block.

From The Kansas City Star,

April 26, 1939:

No. 575

No caption published.

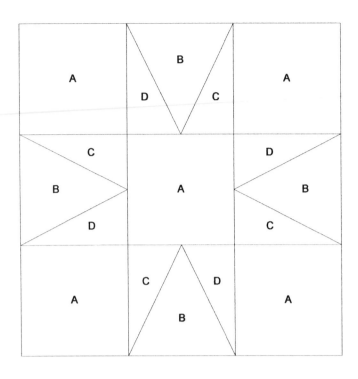

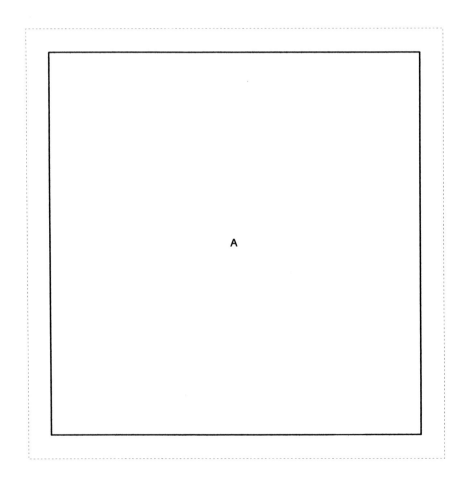

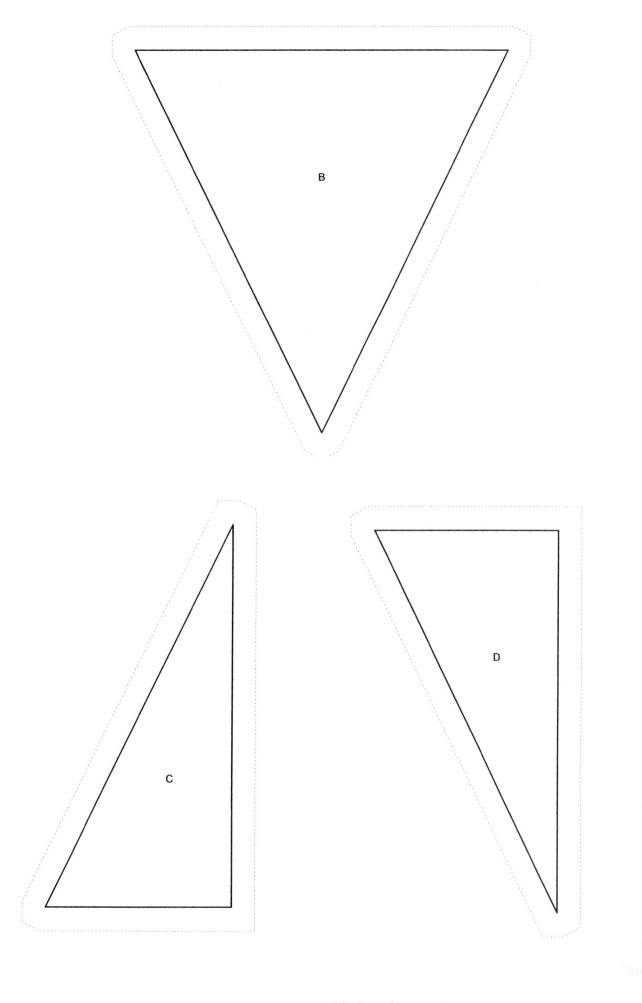

Gold Fish

Block Size: 12" finished

Fabric needed:
Light blue
Medium blue
Gold
Brown
Medium brown

We will be using templates for this block.

From the medium brown fabric, cut
1 – 4 3/8" square. Cut the square from corner to corner once on the diagonal or cut 2 triangles using template A.

From the medium blue fabric, cut
1 – 4 3/8" square. Cut the square from corner to corner once on the diagonal or cut 2 triangles using template A.

From the light blue fabric, cut
4 pieces using template C
4 pieces using template E
4 pieces using template B
4 pieces using template D

From the gold fabric, cut
4 diamonds using template H
4 triangles using template F
4 triangles using template I

From the brown fabric, cut
4 diamonds using template G
4 triangles using template F
4 triangles using template I

First Appeared in The Star **December 12, 1931**

To Make the Block

1 Stitch the I triangles to the light blue E pieces as shown. Make 4.

2 Sew the F triangles to the light blue C pieces. Make 4.

3 Sew the G and H diamonds together in pairs. Then sew two pairs together. That makes up half of the center of the block. Sew the two halves together. Don't sew the seam entirely to the end as these will be inset seams.

Gold Fish

Inset the I-E-I units and the F-C-F units.

Inset the B and D light blue diamonds.

Add the A triangles as shown to complete the block.

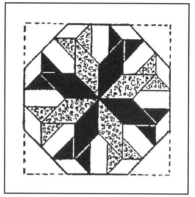

**From The Kansas City Star,
December 12, 1931:**
No. 200

Original size – 17"
This old pattern is a modification of the familiar "Dove in the Window" design. It makes a lovely cushion as well as a quilt, the goldfish are to be in yellow and the surrounding blocks in the pale green of the fish bowl or in any combination of colors. Allow for seams. The block may have eight sides or it may be square as one likes. If used for a pillow, use a strip three or four inches wide to box in the design.

**From The Kansas City Star,
December 10, 1935:**
No. 396

This is a requested pattern by the weekly star's quilt fans. It has many names, the oldest being "Dove in the Window." Gold Fish is a later name. Allow for seams.

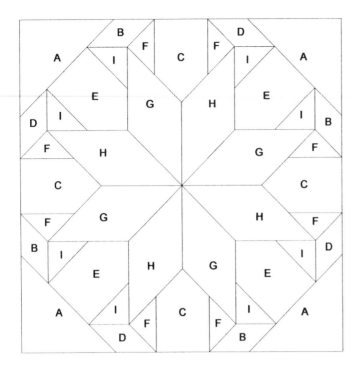

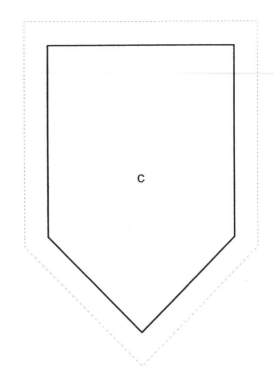

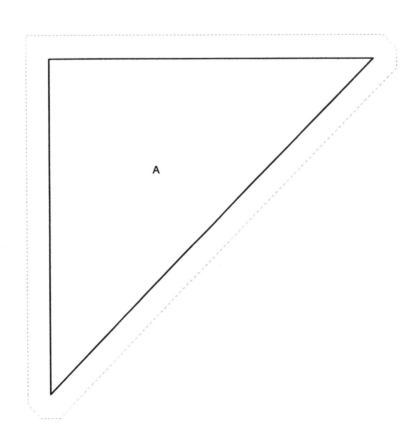

Goldfish

Template

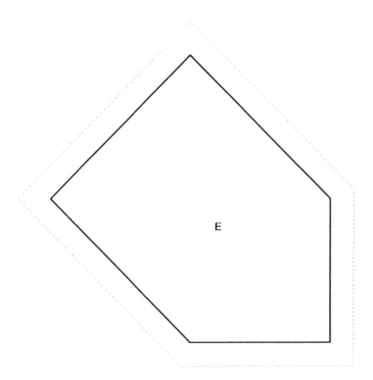

E

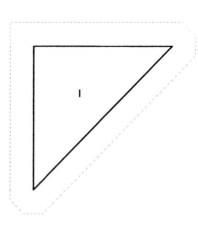

I

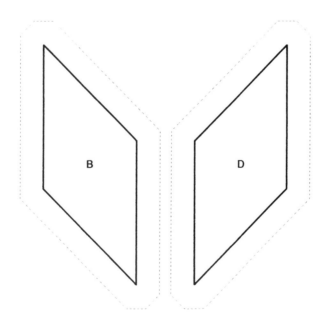

B

D

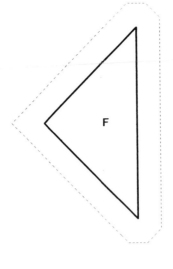

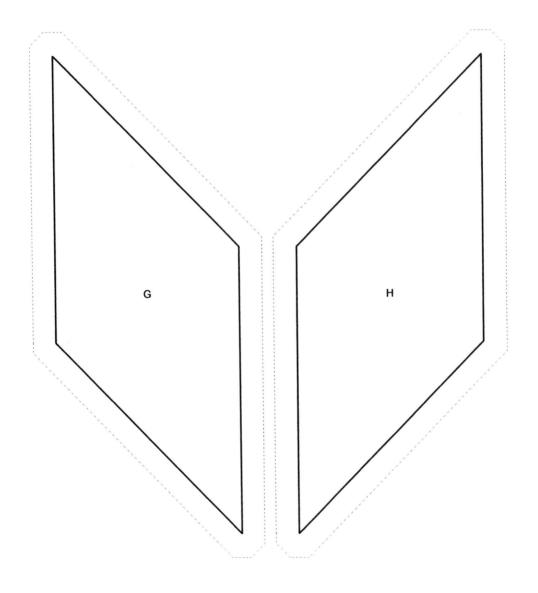

Gold Fish

Template

Submitted by Wanita Morrow, Osceola, Mo. Given to Wanita from her grandmother,
Viola Wrieden Morrow, in the 1970s. Quiltmaker unknown.

English Flower Garden

Block Size: 12" finished

Here's a block for the appliqué enthusiasts.

Fabric needed:

13 1/2" square of **background fabric.** Trim to 12 1/2" when appliqué work is complete.

Assorted **scraps of green** for stems and leaves

Scraps of pink plaids for flowers

Plaid or striped fabric for pot

Dark pink for flower centers.

Cutting Directions

4 leaves using templates B, C, F and G

1 long stem using template H

2 short stems using templates D and E. If you would prefer, you can make bias strips using a 1/4" or 3/8" Clover Bias Tape maker.

From the pink plaid fabrics, cut

3 flowers using templates I, N and K

From the dark pink, cut

flower centers using templates L, O and J

From the plaid or striped fabric, cut

1 flower pot using template M

Appeared in The Star **April 5, 1930**

To Make the Block

1 Fold the background fabric in half vertically and horizontally. Lightly finger press the creases into the fabric in both directions to help with placement.

Pin the pieces in place tucking the ends under another piece when possible. For example, you'll want to make sure the ends of the leaves are behind the stem, the ends of the stems should be tucked under the flowers, etc. Appliqué in place using your favorite method.

From The Kansas City Star,
April 5, 1930:

No. 91

Original size - 16"

A quilt which is as picturesquely English as Ann Hathaway's cottage is this quaint Flower Garden applique. It may be made of all variegated flowers in gay prints with yellow centers, or a color plan of coral, turquoise and gold flowers with green leaves and centers would be lovely. The pot is of green and white check gingham with 16-inch square background blocks of white or light yellow. Twenty blocks, set together with 3-inch strips of green check in lattice effect makes a center about 73x89 inches. A 5-inch border all around this brings it to generous size, both to cover pillows and tuck in at the foot. Seams are not allowed.

History of the Block

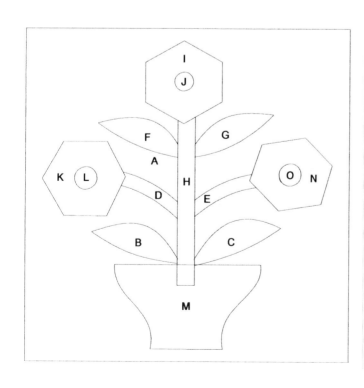

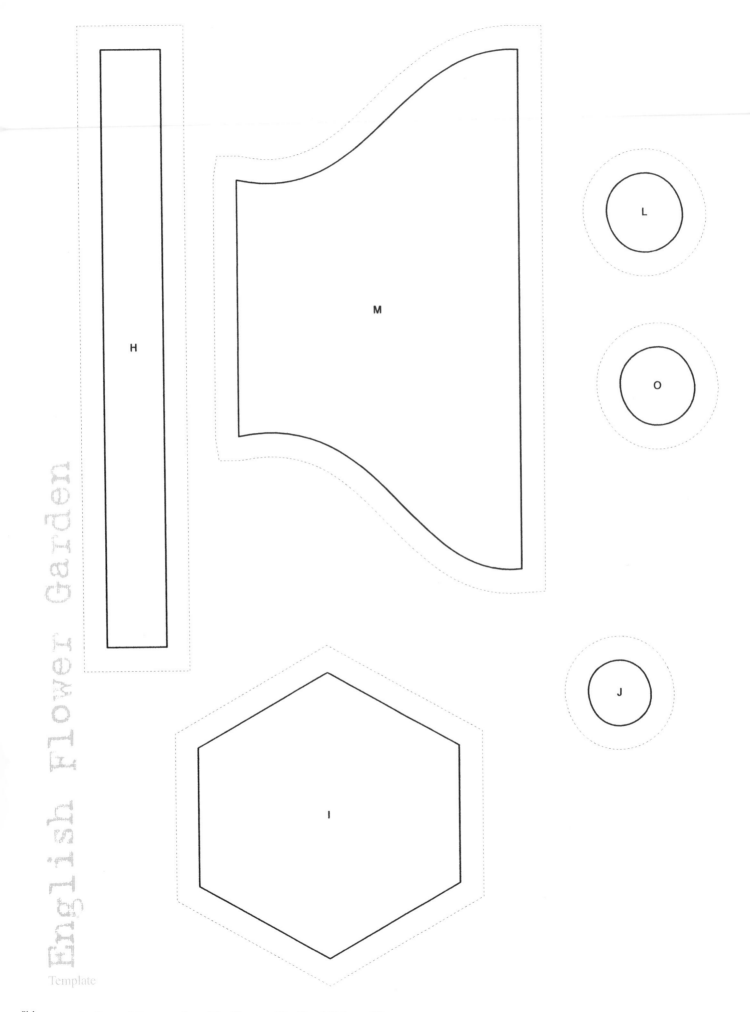

English Flower Garden

Template

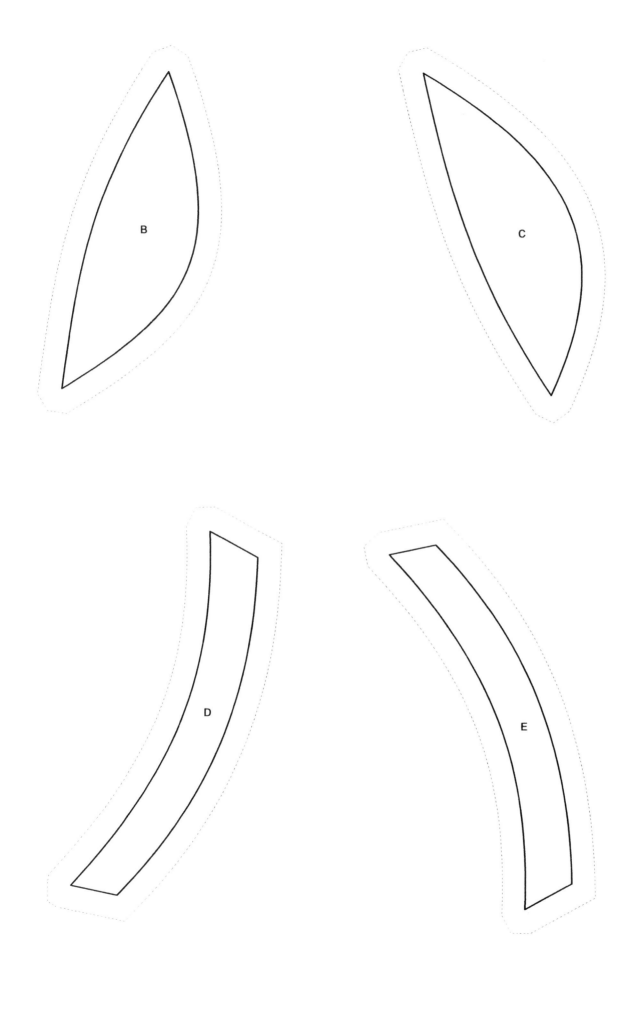

English Flower Garden

Template

F

G

K

N

First appeared in The Star **September 9, 1933**

To Make the Block

1 Sew the tan A triangles to the medium dark green A triangles. You will have 4 half-square triangles.

2 Sew the tan C and B triangles to a dark green E triangle. Make 4.

3 Sew the pieces into rows as shown.

Sew the rows together to complete the block.

Cypress

Block Size: 12" finished

Fabric needed

Dark green

Medium dark green

Tan

The B, C and E pieces in this block come out with some odd measurements so we will be using templates

Cutting Directions

From the dark green, cut

1 square using template D

4 triangles using template E

From the medium dark green, cut

4 triangles using template A

From the tan, cut

4 triangles using template A

4 triangles using template B

4 triangles using template C

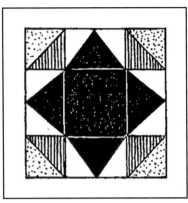

From The Kansas City Star,

September 9, 1933

No. 322

This design may be done in the actual colors of the bright red little flower so familiar to this section of the country. However, it is a design which may be used in other colors as well. Allow for seams.

March 9, 1960

No. 1044

For those who choose the Cypress for a quilt block, a rich reward is promised in finished beauty and easy joining. Amelia Lampton, Aguilar, Colo., the contributor, says the colors named for the pieces are merely suggestions. The maker may choose color combination to please her individual taste.

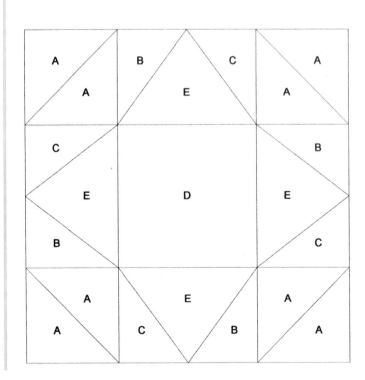

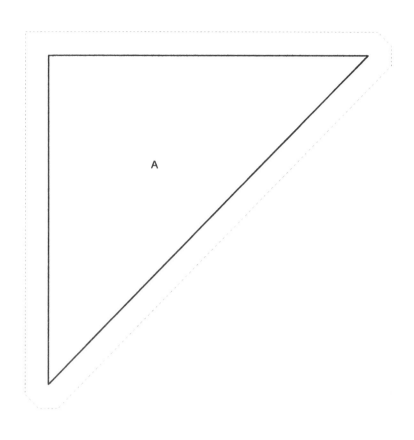

A

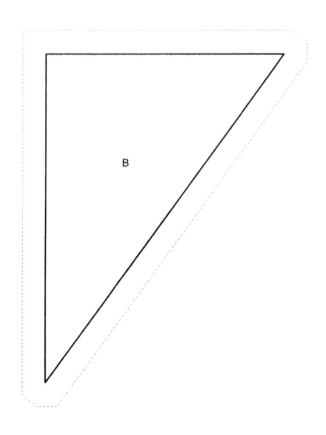

B

Cypress

Template

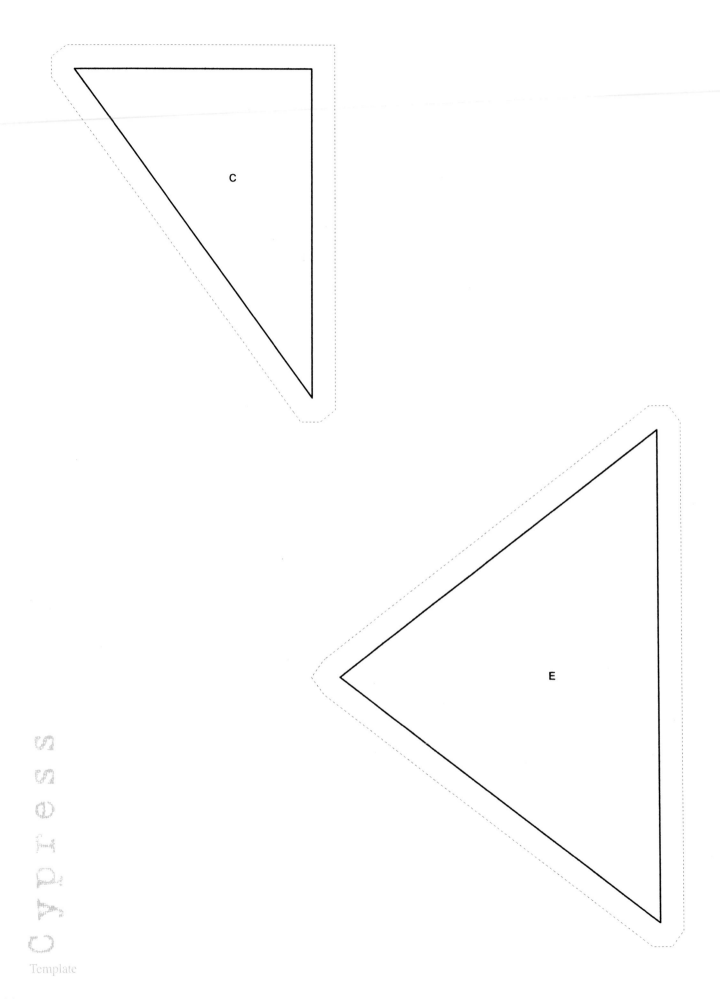

C

E

Cypress

Template

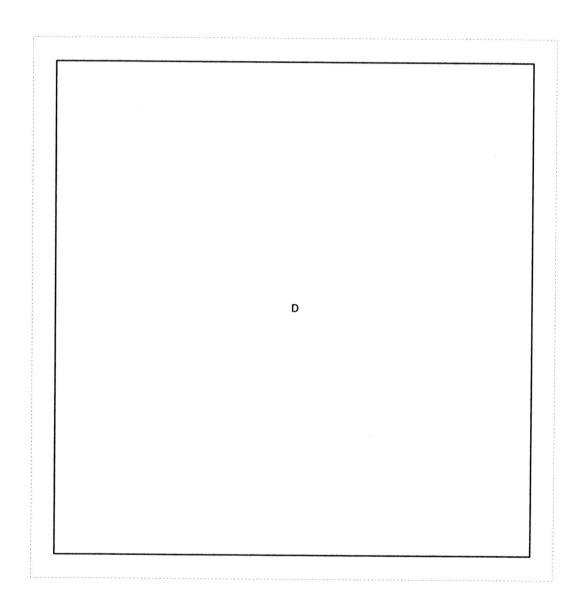

D

To Make the Block

Stitch the E and D diamonds together into pairs as shown. These will be inset seams.

Sew the pairs together to make two halves of the center star. These will be inset seams.

Sew the two halves together. These will be inset seams.

Make a corner unit by sewing the H and F diamonds into pairs. Sew two pairs together. These will be inset seams.

Add the G triangle and inset the B triangles and an A square. Make 4 of these corner units.

Blazing Star

Block Size: 12" finished

Fabric Needed

Double pink print

Green print

Light tan

For precision, we'll use templates for this difficult block.

Cutting Instructions

From the light tan, cut

4 – 2 1/2" squares or use template A

8 triangles using template B

4 pieces using template C

4 triangles using template G

From the double pink, cut

8 diamonds using template F

4 diamonds using template E

From the green print, cut

8 diamonds using template H

4 diamonds using template D

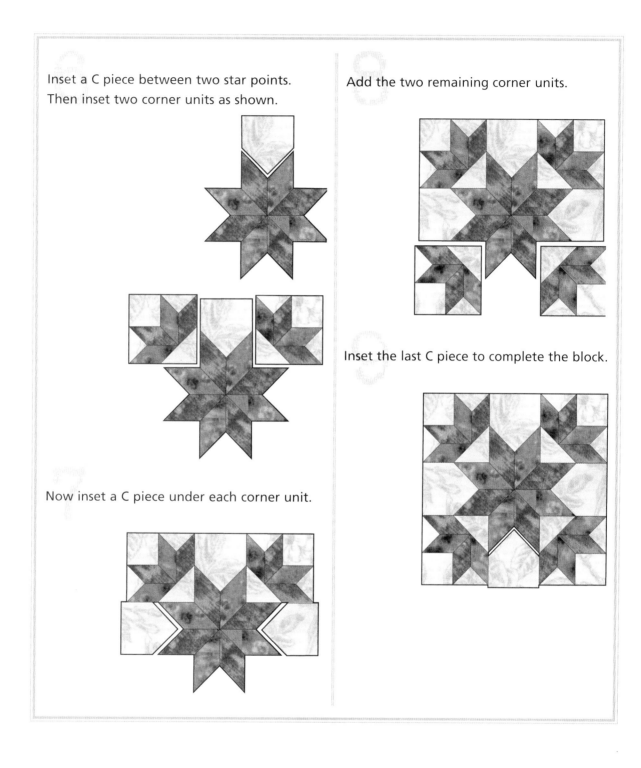

Inset a C piece between two star points. Then inset two corner units as shown.

Now inset a C piece under each corner unit.

Add the two remaining corner units.

Inset the last C piece to complete the block.

**From The Kansas City Star,
February 15, 1930:**
No. 84

"The Blazing Star" is an extremely interesting block in three colors. If one cared to carry out this idea, red, yellow and white would be the most effective. However, the block would be beautiful in a combination of solid colors and a figured background of three pastel colors - pink, blue and a lavender background for example. In piecing this block it would be well to do the four corners first, then the white patches between these squares, joining the two diamond shaped patches at the top. The rest is a simple matter. This block, when complete, is 13-1/2 inches square. Seams are not allowed on these patterns.

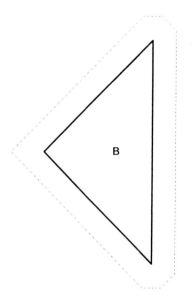

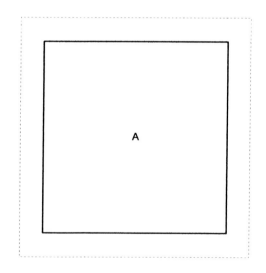

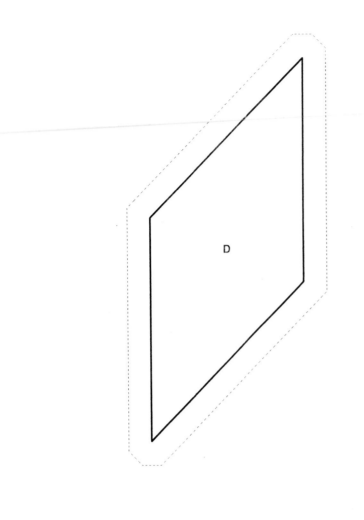

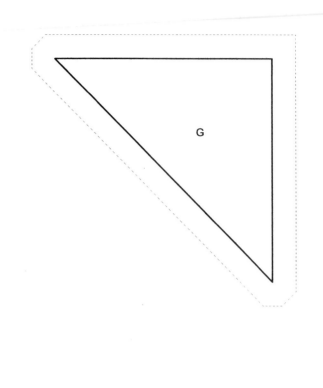

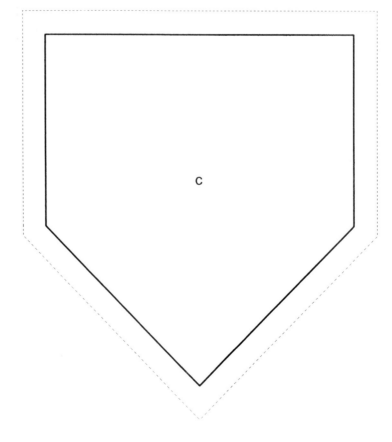

Blazing Star

Template

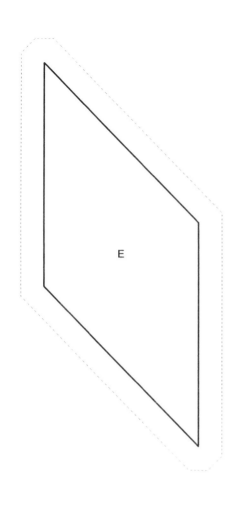

E

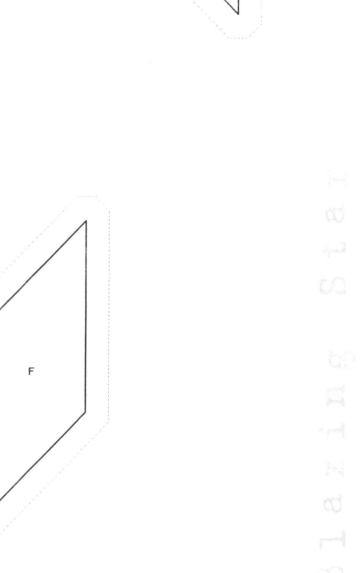

H

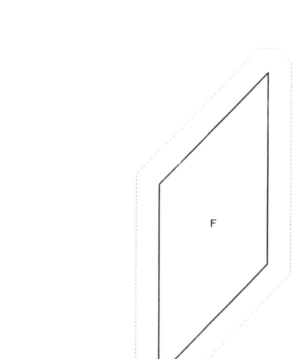

F

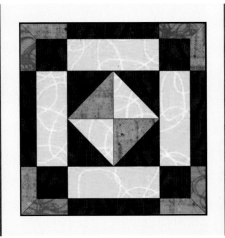

Fair and Square

Block Size: 12" finished

Fabric Needed:

Brown

Gold

Orange

Cutting Directions

From the brown fabric, cut

4 – 1 1/2" x 6 1/2" rectangles or use template B

4 – 2 1/2" squares or use template D

2 – 3 7/8" squares or 4 triangles using template F

From the gold fabric, cut

4 - 2 1/2" x 6 1/2" rectangles or use template E

1 - 3 7/8" square or 2 triangles using template F

From the orange fabric, cut

1 – 3 7/8" square or 2 triangles

using template F

4 pieces using template A

4 pieces using template C

To Make the Block

1 If you cut squares from the brown and gold or orange fabrics, draw a line from corner to corner on the diagonal on the reverse side of the lightest colored fabric. Place a light square atop a brown square with right sides facing and sew 1/4" on either side of the line. Using your rotary cutter, cut on the line. Open each of the half-square triangle units and press toward the dark fabric.

If you chose to cut the triangles using template F, sew a brown triangle to an orange triangle. Make two half-square triangles like this. Then make two more by sewing a brown triangle to a gold triangle. Make two. You should have a total of 4 half-square triangles.

Sew the half-square triangles together as shown to make the center of the block.

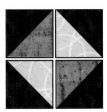

2 Now sew a brown square to either end of a gold rectangle. Make two.

Sew a gold rectangle to either side of the center square.

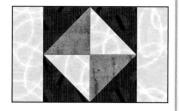

Sew the three rows together.

Sew an orange A and C piece to either end of a brown B rectangle. The mitered edges of the A and C pieces should always angle toward the outside of the block. Make four. The orange A and C pieces are to be inset.

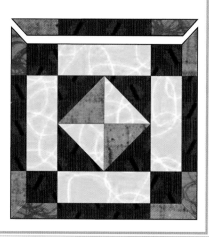

From The Kansas City Star, March 19, 1938:

No. 540

A quilt block designed from a printed handkerchief. All blocks are made with the same prevailing colors. Blue used all through the quilt of the same shade makes a 12-1/2 inch block and takes twenty-one blocks to make a quilt.

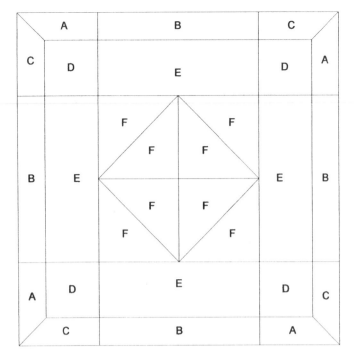

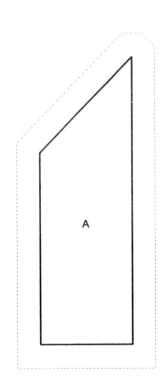

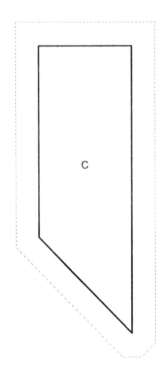

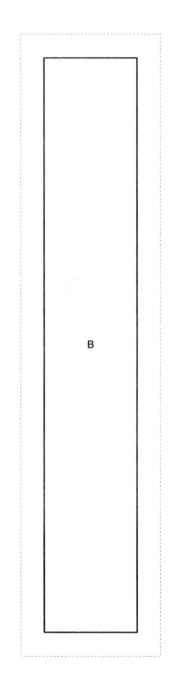

Template

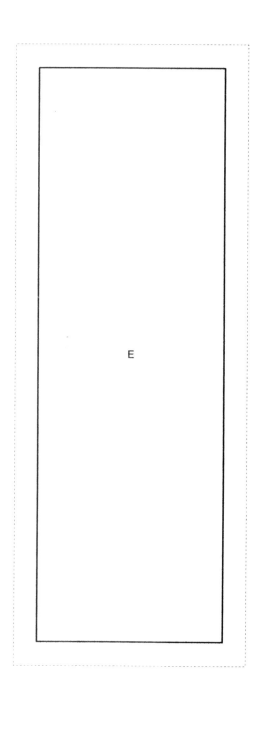

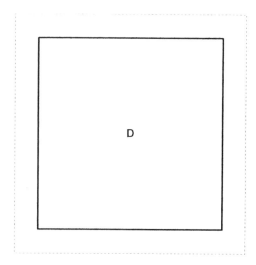

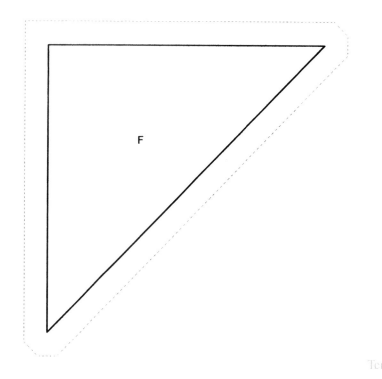

Fair and Square

Template

Grape Basket

Block Size: 11 7/8"

finished

Fabric Needed:

Cream

Light purple

Dark purple

Light green

Dark green

To Make the Block

Make two flying geese units by sewing a light purple B triangle and a dark purple B triangle to the two cream colored C triangles as shown.

Make half-square triangle units by sewing the following triangles together.

2 half-square triangles using cream and light purple

2 half-square triangles using light and dark purple

Cutting Directions

From the cream fabric, cut

1 – 2 7/8" square (template A)

2 rectangles using template D

1 triangle using template E

2 triangles using template C

5 triangles using template B

From the light purple fabric, cut

6 triangles using template B

1 triangle using template E

From the dark purple fabric, cut

4 triangles using template B

From the light green fabric, cut

3 triangles using template B

From the dark green fabric, cut

1 triangle using template E

2 triangles using template B

3 using light green and cream

You'll also need to make one half-square triangle using the light purple and the dark green E triangles.

Sew the top row of the basket together as shown. You should have a square, a half-square triangle and a flying geese unit.

The second row is made up of half-square triangles sewn together as shown below.

Now sew the remaining flying geese unit to two half-square triangles. Add these to the large purple and green half-square triangle.

Sew the rows you have made so far together as shown.

Sew the green B triangles to the cream rectangles as shown. Sew one to each side of the basket.

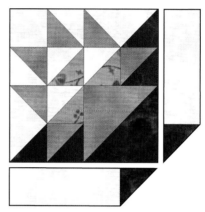

Sew the remaining cream triangle to the base of the basket to complete the block.

**From The Kansas City Star,
March 8, 1930:**

No. 87

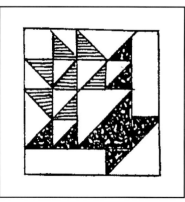

Basket quilts are always popular. Here are several charming versions easy to piece. The main part of this one is a 4-patch of pieced squares as indicated by the extended lines. To this the long strips with a small triangle on the ends are added, then the final bottom triangle to complete. The grape basket completes into a block ten inches square if seams are added to the unit patterns here given. It should be set together on the diagonal with alternate plain squares and half squares of white to the edges. Twenty-five blocks plus a 6-inch border and binding makes a full sized quilt.

History of the Block

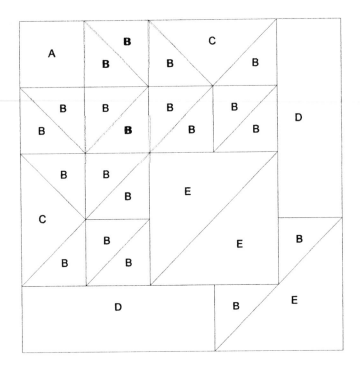

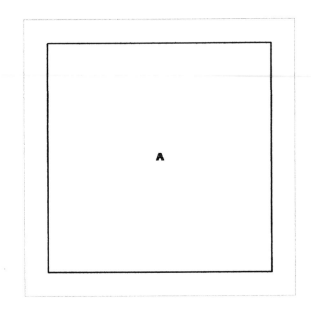

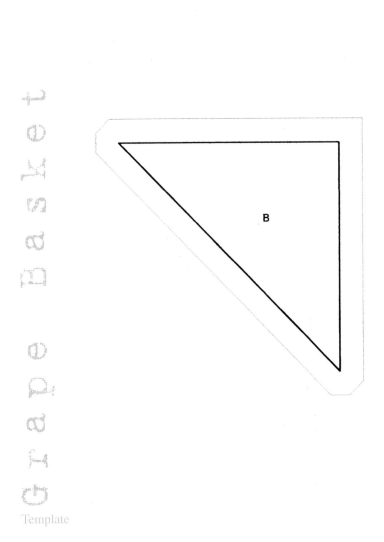

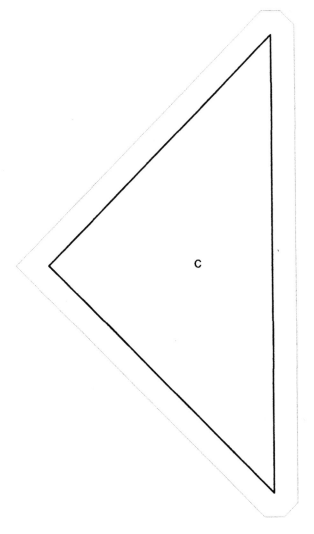

Grape Basket

Template

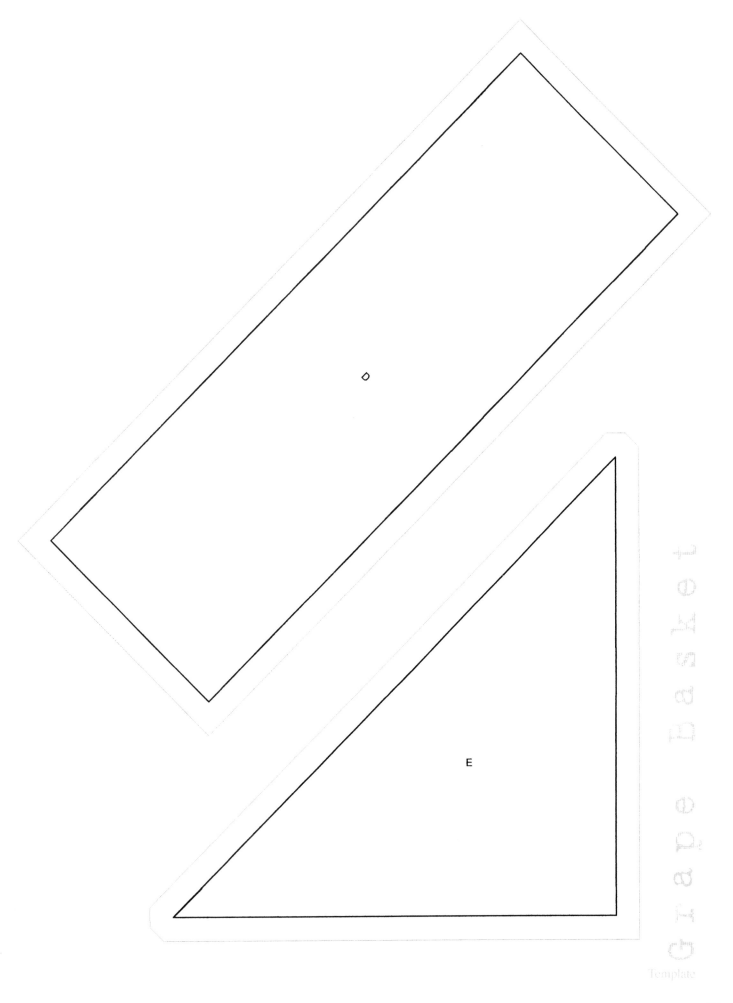

D

E

Grape Basket

Template

Happy Nap by Nancy Mathewson, Weaverville, NC. Designed and quilted by Nancy Mathewson.

Appeared in The Star **April 4, 1945**

To Make the Block

Sew the tan plaid A pieces to the tan plaid B pieces. Make 4.

Sew a red A piece to a red B piece. Make 4.

Sew a red plaid AB unit to a tan plaid AB unit. Add a light tan C triangle to either side. Make two.

Sew a red plaid AB unit to a tan plaid AB unit. Add a small plaid C triangle to either side. Make two.

Scottish Cross

Block Size: 12" finished

Fabric Needed:
Red plaid
Tan plaid
Small plaid
Tan print
Light tan

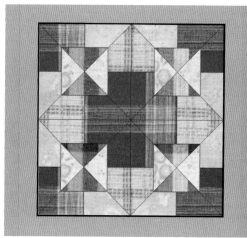

Odd sizes and shapes make this block a perfect candidate for templates.

Cutting Directions
From the small plaid, cut
2 – 4 1/4" squares. Cut the squares from corner to corner twice on the diagonal to make 8 C triangles or use template C.

From the light tan fabric, cut
2 – 4 1/4" squares. Cut the squares from corner to corner twice on the diagonal to make 8 C triangles or use template C.

From the red plaid fabric, cut
8 pieces using template A
8 pieces using template B

From the tan plaid fabric, cut
4 pieces using template A
4 pieces using template B

From the tan print fabric, cut
4 pieces using template A
4 pieces using template B

Scottish Cross

Sew the four units together to make the center of the block as shown.

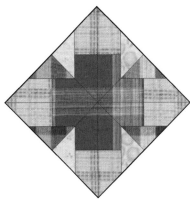

Sew the remaining red plaid A and B pieces to the tan A and B pieces. You should have four strips that look like this.

And four strips that look like this.

Add a small plaid triangle to four of the strips so you will have four ABC units like this.

Now sew a light tan C triangle to the remaining strips, making four ABC units like this.

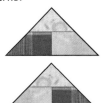 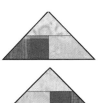

Sew the corner units together as shown. Make 4.

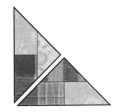 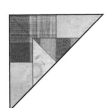

 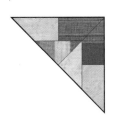

Sew the corner units to the center of the block.

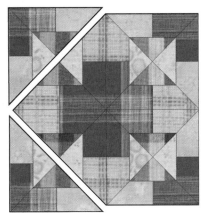

From The Kansas City Star,

April 4, 1945:

No. 763

Very effective is this design in
its use of white and dark 1-tone
pieces, combined with plain and
print triangles. Mrs. Chester F.
Duncan, Route 1, Carson, Ia., is
the designer.

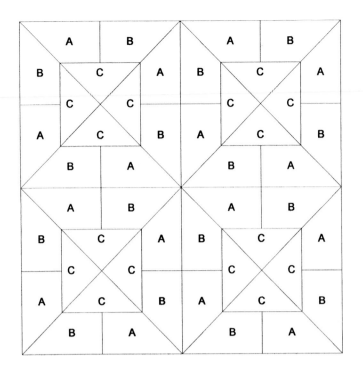

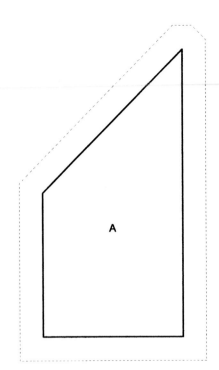

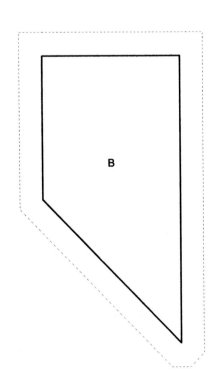

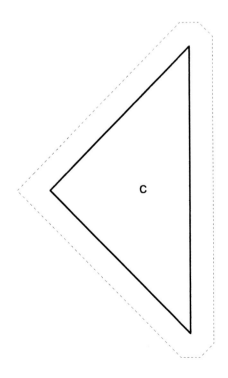

Appeared in The Star **June 19, 1940**

Garden Walk

Block Size: 12" finished

Fabric Needed:

Dark green

Rose

Cream

To Make the Block

1 If you cut 2 1/2" squares from the cream and rose fabrics, sew them together into 4-patch units. If you cut the strips, sew them together horizontally then cut the strip into 2 1/2" increments. Make five 4-patch units.

2 Sew a green D triangle and a green C triangle to either side of a cream B triangle. Make four.

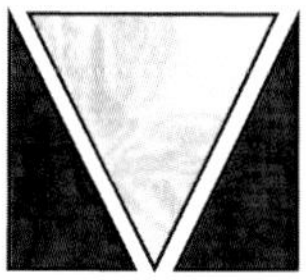

3 Sew the 4-patch units and the triangle units together into rows as shown below.

Sew the rows together to complete the block

Cutting Directions

From the dark green, cut

4 triangles using template C

4 triangles using template D

From the cream fabric, cut

1 – 26" x 2 1/2" strip or cut 10 – 2 1/2" squares

(template A)

4 triangles using template B

From the rose fabric, cut

1 – 26" x 2 1/2" strip or cut 10 – 2 1/2" squares

(template A)

Garden Walk

From The Kansas City Star,

June 19, 1940:

No. 619

"This quilt is lovely," says Mrs. George R. Kennedy, Hunter, Ark., the contributor, "if the 'stepping' blocks are made of blue, and the triangular pieces of print in a mixture of pink, lavender and yellow."

A	A	B		A	A
A	A	D	C	A	A
	C	A	A		D
B		A	A		B
	D	A	A		C
A	A	C	D	A	A
A	A	B		A	A

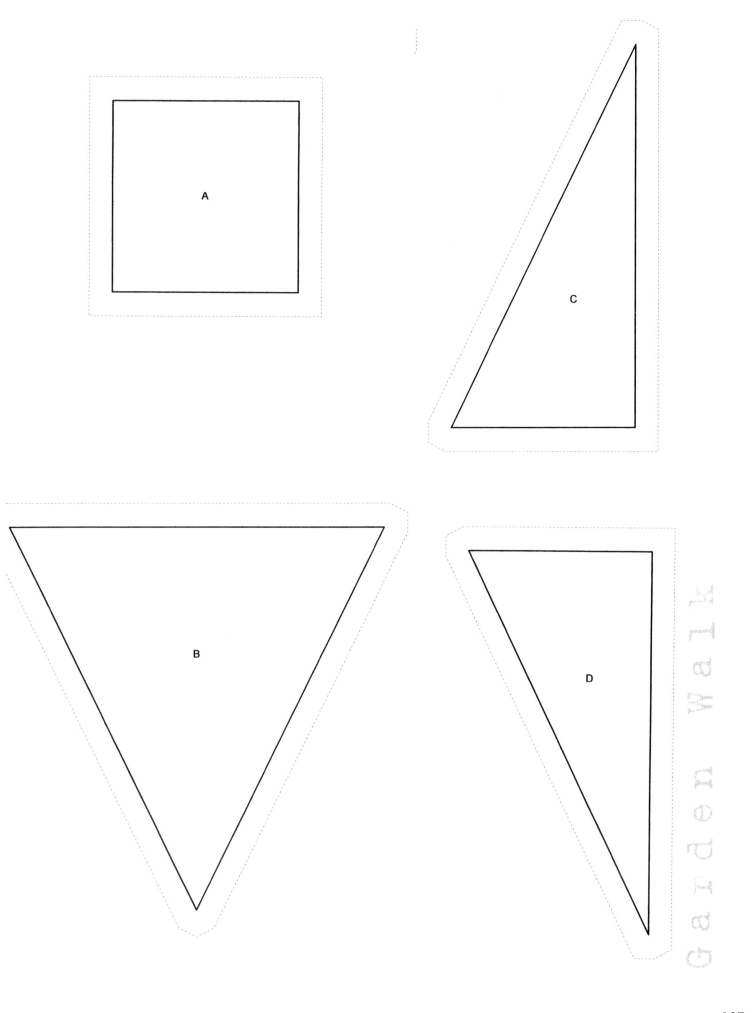

A

C

B

D

Garden Walk

Stars Abound by Charlotte O'Leary, Fruitland, Idaho. Designed and sewn by Charlotte O'Leary.
Quilted by David and SueAnn Suderman, Heirloom Quilting Studio, Salem, Ore.

Appeared in The Star **December 27, 1939**

To Make the Block

If you cut 2 1/2" squares from the cream and blue fabrics, sew them together into 4-patch units. If you cut the strips, sew them together horizontally then cut the strip into 2 1/2" increments. Make four 4-patch units.

Sew the squares and 4-patch units into rows.

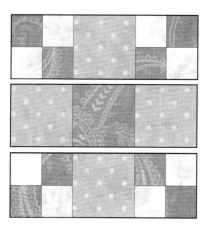

Thrifty

Block Size: 12" finished

Fabric Needed:

Cream

Blue

Pink

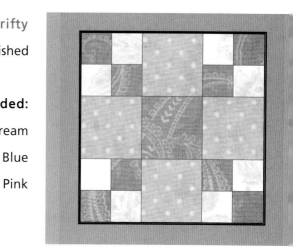

This is an easy block that can be cut using a rotary cutter and ruler.

Cutting Directions

From the cream fabric, cut

1 – 21" x 2 1/2" strip or cut 8 – 2 1/2" squares

(template A)

From the blue fabric, cut

1 – 21" x 2 1/2" strip or cut 8 – 2 1/2" squares

(template A)

1 – 4 1/2" square (template B)

From the pink fabric, cut

4 – 4 1/2" squares (template B)

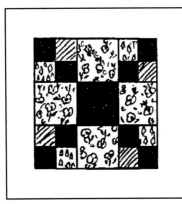

From The Kansas City Star,

December 27, 1939:

No. 602

The idea for the Thrifty design originated by Mrs. Clarence Welker, Millersville, Mo. She chose this name for the pattern because she went to her scrap bag for the three kinds of print and the 1-tone pieces required for it.

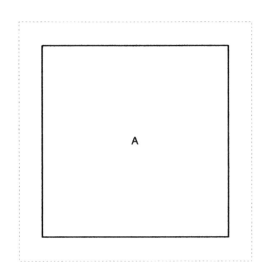

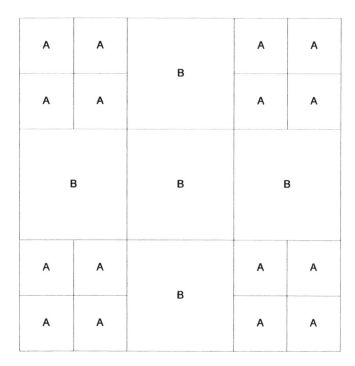

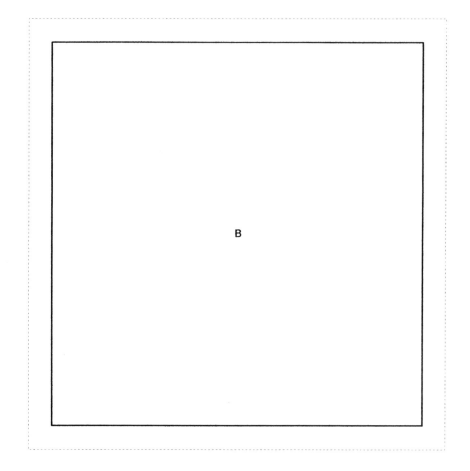